50 DRAMATISED BIBLE READINGS

50 Dramatised Bible Readings

DAVID BURT

EASTBOURNE

ISBN 1 84291 039 6

Published by
KINGSWAY COMMUNICATIONS LTD
Lottbridge Drove, Eastbourne BN23 6NT, England.
Email: books@kingsway.co.uk

Book design and production for the publishers by
Bookprint Creative Services, P.O. Box 827, BN21 3YJ, England.
Printed in Great Britain.

For Sue

Contents

NEW TESTAMENT

CONTENTS

Prologue

So, there you are, sitting in church and everything is going pretty much as normal. The minister has welcomed his flock with some suitable words of encouragement, garnished with a generous dash of repartee; songs have been sung, prayers have been prayed and the velvet collection pouch has been furtively passed around the congregation.

There's even been a highly energetic action chorus led by the Sunday school; and their intrepid leader, Miss Wiston, has attempted to explain the triune nature of God to the little darlings, aided only by an empty Weetabix box, a toilet roll and a Dyson vacuum cleaner! Work that one out if you can.

It is now with a sense of muted anticipation that the congregation await the main course of a fifty-minute sermon, delivered with the familiar charm of the silver-tongued preacher. Just before this treat, however, a designated member of the congregation rises and nervously takes the long walk from her seat to the lofty heights of the pulpit. Yes, you've got it: it's time for the Scripture reading.

The reading itself only takes about two minutes, and everybody agrees that a jolly good job has been done. This is confirmed by the encouraging smiles and nods aimed at the brave volunteer as she hastily returns to the safety of her seat. Not a single word was mispronounced or stumbled over, including the infuriating minor prophet whose name seems to consist of about thirty-seven letters.

The only problem is that during the silent pause between the end of the reading and the beginning of the sermon, the congregation begin collectively to realise that they haven't got the slightest clue what the reading was about. It was perhaps rather monotone, but on the whole read very well, and everyone was listening attentively, yet somehow the meaning of the passage has totally eluded them.

Perhaps even more worryingly, the meaning completely eluded the reader too!

Introduction

Okay, so I admit that maybe in my silly little prologue I have been prone to a small degree of exaggeration – call it poetic licence if you will. But I wonder if there is any hint of familiarity in that scenario when you compare it to the reading of Scripture in your own church.

I'm sure we can all agree that the reading of Scripture in a church service is an essential rather than an optional element and should be given a place of due importance and regard. In the pages of the Old Testament we hear about public readings of Scripture and what a key role they played in the life of the people of God. Yet in practice today it seems often to occupy a nominal supporting role, usually a two-minute precursor to a lengthy sermon. Worse still is my personal pet hate of a reading being split up and expounded on one verse at a time, so the congregation never even hear it read as a whole.

I'm not taking some moral high ground here, accusing everyone of not giving due precedence to the importance of the Scriptures. If I were doing that, the first place I would aim the critical glance would be at myself. I'm in no doubt that church leaders and members everywhere are committed to utilise the Scriptures in church as positively as possible. The question is, how best can we do this? What methods can we employ to make the reading both exciting and central to our meetings? At the heart of these questions is the reason behind the origin of this book. My desire is to see the Scriptures communicated clearly and powerfully in church, not *instead of* inspired preaching, but *in addition to* and in partnership with it.

In the following pages I have set out fifty popular Bible passages in script format, giving guidelines and various ideas that I have used to help make the readings come alive. Although I speak of dramatised readings, and my previous books have been originally conceived sketches, all the selections in this book are pure Scripture and will not waiver a single word from the biblical text. The Bible is the greatest story ever told, with enough drama to keep the most discerning listener enthralled. To communicate this powerfully we do not need to change its content, just the way we deliver or present it. When we consider reading the Bible in church, we should regard it, as with so many other acts of service, as an important act of worship.

I believe that if just a small percentage of the time and effort we put into preaching a sermon or organising the worship were employed when preparing a Bible reading, the results would be potentially astounding.

I recently heard on the radio a startling statistic, stating how fewer and fewer Christians regularly read the Bible as part of their personal devotions. How tragic that a practice so central to our faith is in such decline. Yet if we do not appear to give it due priority in our services, church members might understandably not see or realise its importance.

My hope is that in some way some of the ideas in this book will help to encourage powerful readings, enthusing and strengthening the church body.

Common Pitfalls

To begin with I want to look at four common pitfalls which lead to the Scriptures not being communicated effectively, thus confusing or, worse still, being totally misunderstood by the congregation. As I go through these, please don't assume that I'm some super-organised supremo who gets it spot on every time; the only reason I'm aware of these pitfalls is because at one time or another I've fallen posterior first into all of them! I'm also fully aware that time constraints are often a factor in preparing services and that we can occasionally be forced to cut corners. In a reasonably ideal world, however, these are the things we should commonly be most aware of.

1. Not given priority

This is as much an attitude we have as an action we need to take. I may be alone here, but often it seems that so many other things in a meeting take precedence over the actual reading of Scripture. It's not that any of these other things are wrong, but sometimes it feels as if it's all a bit out of balance. If we're honest, in most churches reading the notices takes up twice as much time as reading the Scriptures. Obviously the notices need to be given – if Daphne arrived on the wrong day for the women's action group, the whole life of the church would grind to a halt – but surely the balance should give us pause for thought.

Preaching the word is, in the main, seen as the central part of teaching in the service. I remember a speaker coming to my church many years ago and turning the whole thing on its head. Instead of reading a short passage then preaching on it for half an hour or so, as is the norm, he totally switched the balance, reading a huge passage of Scripture and then finishing off with a five-minute talk. Now I think that's taking the idea a bit too far as there is only so much Scripture we can take in at a single sitting, but I did find his approach quite inspirational. Although he may have taken his point to an extreme, is it any more of an extreme than half-heartedly reading about a dozen verses and then lecturing on them for fifty minutes? There must be a balance somewhere, in which both reading the word and preaching the word are given their due place.

Let me pause here, before I dig myself a big hole, to assure you that I am in no way anti-preaching. Quite the opposite, in fact: I absolutely love it, whether doing it or listening to it. I imagine one of the best parts of a minister's job is having the opportunity to preach every week. There's nothing like learning from the Scriptures, listening to what God is saying to you through them and then thinking of ways to communicate that creatively to a congregation. Of course, I'm not a minister and don't imagine I ever will be! However much I'd enjoy that part of the job, anyone who knows me will tell you that the more delicate and 'political' aspects of the role are not among the giftings God has graciously granted me.

As I've said before, it's not about giving the Scripture reading priority at the expense of preaching or anything else, but in addition to it. Whoever is reading the word should be encouraged that it is an essential part of the service. Without it, preaching the word will not be put into its proper context.

But with this ideal also comes a responsibility for the leader. It's very common for someone to be asked to do the reading ten minutes before the start of the service. They probably agree to do it reluctantly and slope off to a quiet corner to run it through in their heads, making sure they know all the words and fervently praying it's not chock full of long, difficult place names. This, of course, is vaguely ridiculous and gives the reader little chance of communicating the meaning of the passage. They might speak it very clearly, but that's a different thing to understanding it.

So when I say we should give priority to reading the word, I don't mean that we should be purists, insisting that it's the longest part of the meeting at the expense of everything else. I mean that it should simply be seen as a key part of the service and not merely a token two-minute gesture, prepared in a haphazard manner at the final hour.

2. Not properly practised

'I haven't had time to practise . . .'
'Oooh, I forgot I was doing it this week . . .'
'I was only asked to do it ten minutes ago . . .'

These are just a few of the classic excuses people give when manically skimming through a Scripture passage, minutes before reading it to the congregation. In the previous pitfall I touched on the problem of an individual being given no notice to prepare; in this section I am assuming that prior notice has been given.

When reading Scripture in front of a congregation it is essential to practise it in advance, yet so often the reader's first vocalisation of the passage is in front of a packed church. In my work I am used to regular public speaking and enjoy it very much. Even with this experience, however, I wouldn't choose to speak cold to an audience without planning at least roughly what to say. In my opinion, not to plan or practise shows disrespect to your listeners. When an audience of any kind sits and listens to someone, they have the right to expect that the person has planned what they are doing. Of course, at times you're dropped in it and have to wing it as best you can, but given the choice that is to be avoided at all costs. It amazes me how many people clearly do not practise in advance of speaking the word. Obviously, there are sometimes genuine reasons; we don't live in an ideal world. But often it's either laziness or innocently thinking that it makes little difference whether you have practised or not. I can assure you that it very definitely does make a difference.

The biggest giveaway of an unrehearsed reading is when the reader pauses in all the wrong places. This may seem like a minor thing, but it can completely change the meaning of a piece of writing. As long as you have read the passage out loud a few times in advance, that particular pitfall is very easily avoided. The worst culprits, believe it or not, are often preachers, and I can confess to this from personal experience. I also think I have a good idea why the error is made.

When planning a sermon on a specific passage, you can spend literally hours poring over the same few verses, and it can feel as if you know them back to front and upside down. Your understanding of them will certainly be excellent by the time you've finished, but when you come to reading the same verses out loud it can be a totally different thing. However well you know the reading in your head, it is essential to read it out loud to make sure you get the phrasing correct.

A similar discipline applies in acting, when performers attempt to commit their lines to memory. You can be sure you know the words to perfection in your head (having rehearsed them over and over on the bus, in the loo and just about every waking moment), but as soon as you vocalise them, they seem to take on a different form and you instantly forget them. Words learnt to perfection in the head are not the same as words learnt to perfection in speech. So, always run through a reading out loud, not just in your head.

It may seem as if I'm going overboard, suggesting that you rehearse the lines as if you were performing a full-scale drama. I don't think it's necessary to learn the lines off by heart, but in order to communicate as effectively as possible I do believe it's important to be so familiar with the text that you know what's coming next. Reading a bunch of words is very different from communicating a truth or telling a story. I won't be trite and say that practice makes perfect, but I promise you that it will make all the difference to the understanding of the listeners whom you are serving.

3. Not properly understood

This again may seem a bit on the obvious side, but it is a common pitfall. Unless readers have a pretty good general understanding of what they are reading, it will be virtually impossible for them to communicate the meaning to their listeners. Vocalising a collection of words, however nicely you may do it, is once again a very different thing from communicating a truth or telling a story.

In the past few years I have had the privilege of sitting on judging panels for both West End and regional theatre award schemes. As you can imagine, in this role I have sat through a great many productions of Shakespeare's plays. They have varied from being excellent to frankly dire. In the main, the worst productions are the ones where the audience has no clue what is going on, and in many cases I'm pretty sure the actors don't either! Imagine how ludicrous it would be for a Shakespearean actor to step on stage in front of a capacity audience, spouting the bard's timeless soliloquies, but without the faintest idea what he was talking about. I must admit, even with study the exact meaning of certain lines in certain Shakespeare plays eludes me, but at a very minimum when performing the lines you should know what they basically mean and what emotions they are expressing. Yet you can see it in an actor's eye when he is clueless to the meaning. There's a kind of vacant emptiness. However elegant the actual speaking of the words might be, all that can be communicated to the audience is what the communicator himself understands, which in some cases is next to nothing.

We can apply these same guidelines to the understanding and reading of the Scriptures. If we do not understand what we are speaking about, all we will communicate to our listeners is our total confusion. Of course, you can argue that the living word of God is so inspired and powerful that we could read it with a complete lack of expression and understanding, and the Holy Spirit could still do his work on all who were listening; and to a point I would have to agree. However, I don't think this should be used as an excuse for us to negate our responsibility to do the best we can with our God-given talents. If you take this line of reasoning too far, we would end up just letting God do all the work while we put our feet up.

When preparing a reading, therefore, begin by going through it a few times first. This may seem fairly basic, but I guarantee that even doing this, after each read through you will add another layer to your understanding. In addition, I would recommend checking out one of the many Bible commentaries available. I've got quite a few different ones, which vary in style and opinion, and I find it very helpful to compare them to get as clear an understanding as possible.

At the risk of sounding holier than thou, I can honestly say that once you have an understanding of what you are saying, and have coupled that with a well practised delivery, it is a real pleasure and privilege to be in a position not just to read but to truly communicate the word to others. I believe that the reading of the word is as much an act of worship as anything else that happens in a church service, and in our efforts we need to treat it as such.

4. Not put in context

As part of our personal understanding of a Scripture reading, and in some instances our direct communication with a congregation, it is important that we put a verse or passage into its relevant context. I find it very annoying when single verses or short passages of Scripture are quoted and used out of their original context, often undermining what is subsequently spoken about them. Certain passages stand alone more comfortably than others, of course, but that isn't to say they are better or any more important.

To use a couple of obvious examples, John 3:16 is often quoted alone, simply because it gives us the gospel in a nutshell and can't very easily be misunderstood. But do you know to whom Jesus was speaking when he said these words? In general terms it clearly speaks to all mankind, but in Scripture it was spoken to one man. (Check out the passage for the answer to this little teaser!) This is the kind of information that can be discovered when reading through and around a passage. Alternatively, if we quote Matthew 5:38 (eye for eye, tooth for tooth . . .) on its own, we could find ourselves in a whole heap of trouble. It is only when we read down a few verses and understand the overall message of the Sermon on the Mount that we can clearly see what Jesus was trying to communicate. It is therefore important that we put the Scriptures in their context.

The preacher Martyn Lloyd-Jones, who famously delivered long sermons on single words or verses of Scripture, could easily have fallen into this pitfall, but he didn't. When he spoke, however short the phrase he was actually preaching on, he always read the whole passage or section to place it in its context for the congregation. We would be wise to imitate this in order to communicate our chosen passage in the best possible way.

Certainly, as the reader, we should know what happened just before and just after the Scripture we are reading. By simply reading around the passage and dipping into a chosen commentary we can very easily understand the context. In some cases, if you deem it necessary, you can also give a brief explanation of the setting to the congregation. You don't need to deliver a mini-sermon to do this, or tread on the preacher's toes; something very basic will suffice, aiding the listeners to place the setting in their minds. For instance, 'After Paul's second missionary trip to—he penned this letter from his prison cell in—' Nothing fancy, just a basic sentence, but one that can make all the difference to your audience's understanding.

That just about covers the major pitfalls we need to avoid when reading Scripture. They can be summarised in these eight handy hints:

- **Plan ahead.** In advance, pray through and plan who will read and what will be read. Don't leave it until the night before or, even worse, the very last minute.
- **Read it through.** Carefully read through the passage a few times, instantly adding layers to your understanding of the text.
- **Read around the text.** By reading the chapter or chapters just before and after the text, ensure you know what is happening, who is speaking to whom and other general circumstances of the passage.
- **Study a commentary.** Read through your favourite Bible commentary to further increase your understanding of the passage.
- **Read out loud.** Once you have gained a good understand-

ing of the passage, practise reading it out loud. You should never only practise a reading in your head.

- **Learn it.** Don't learn it by heart, but always have a good idea of what's coming next so that you can look up at your audience regularly and deliver the reading with confidence.

- **Put it in context.** Having studied a commentary and understood the general context of the reading for yourself, decide if you think it is necessary to put the passage into some form of context for the listeners, or if this can be communicated by the way you present the reading.

- **Enjoy it!** Having taken the time to understand and prepare the reading properly, pray that your listeners will respond, and then enjoy delivering the powerful word of God.

How to Prepare a Dramatised Reading

Now that you have taken time to avoid the pitfalls and have understood and prepared a polished reading, what other methods can you employ to best communicate the Scriptures? A well spoken piece may not need any embellishments, but I want us to look at some ideas we might use to dramatise the Scriptures, hopefully improving the general understanding of our listeners.

I make no apology for suggesting that the Scriptures need dramatising; as I've said before, we're not changing the text itself, merely the way in which we deliver it. Jesus himself gives us the perfect example of using creative communication methods with visual imagery in his parables. We need to learn from this, varying the approaches we take in communication, or it can all become a bit stilted. A clever shock tactic successfully used once becomes a little bit boring the sixth or seventh time! What keeps a listener interested is something a bit different (without being too off the wall), which makes a passage more easily understood. While their interest is engaged, they are involved. Allow your listeners to lose the thread, however, and you lose their interest and concentration altogether.

There are exceptions to every rule, but we need to learn the rules before we can break them. Jesus often left his spectators scratching their heads in confusion, questions unanswered. In drama I love to do this, allowing an audience to make up their own minds about various issues. In the case of communicating Scripture, however, I think it is important to avoid being cryptic and to keep the reading as crystal clear as possible.

The suggestions that follow won't take a great deal of time to prepare, just the commitment to serve the reading as best you can. It is highly unlikely, and very inadvisable, that you should use all the suggestions in all the readings. Use the list as an ideas factory. The ones you like, use where you can; the ones you don't think would be appropriate, leave out. In the scripts that follow I have given directions, but as individuals and groups adopt personal styles I hope you will use them purely as guidelines, creating readings that suit you best.

1. 'Sorry, I missed that . . .' (Understand it)

No groans please! I know I keep banging on about this, but I really believe that it is one of the key and unrealised reasons why the Scriptures can be misread. There's nothing more painful than listening to someone droning through a reading, totally monotone and with about as much life as a piece of Kentucky fried chicken, but at least this is an upfront and totally apparent fault. If someone has a good speaking voice, it can be easy to cover up the cracks of a total lack of understanding, yet the reading suffers enormously. Simply put, you cannot dramatise anything without first gaining a proper understanding, so don't even try!

2. 'No tongue twisters please . . .' (Speak clearly)

It's another seemingly obvious point, but all too often the planned dramatic reading ends up as nothing more than a meaningless slur. Each word needs to be clearly heard, or the whole thing is a waste of everyone's time. If you're unsure of

the clarity of your diction, ask a friend to listen to you practise and point out any inaudible words or phrases. This can
be a very fruitful exercise and often the problem is something
as simple as slowing down your delivery or being careful not
to drop your Ds and Ts.

Part of speaking clearly is in the tone of your voice. By
varying the tone for narrative and speech, we can define the
difference and avoid mass congregational slumber. Think
about using pauses for effect, but avoid using them too often
or for too long. Some of the sentences in the NIV transla-
tion are very long; it is essential to know when to pause and
where to put the emphasis on the phrase. There's nothing
more embarrassing than dropping your voice at the end of a
sentence, only to realise that there's a bit more left in the
same thought, after a comma. Verbally rehearsing the
reading will make these points very clear.

Remember also to change the volume and intensity of
your voice. When you're having a quiet heart-to-heart discussion with a close friend, you use a different part of your voice
from when you're at the supermarket complaining that your
milk has turned to cheese two days before its sell-by date. I've
no reason to believe that our biblical heroes didn't also
animate their voices, so let's try to recreate that. Use passion,
anger, jealousy, calmness or whatever the text requires to
communicate effectively. It's not necessary to go into a full Al
Pacino-style rant (you don't want to give the old dears in the
back row a heart attack) but understand and use the emotion
of a piece to demonstrate its meaning clearly.

3. 'I wanna tell you a story . . .' (Tell the story)

You know that feeling when you're at a dinner party or some
other social gathering and the topic of conversation conveniently turns to a topic on which you have a great story to
share? You await a suitable lull in conversation and then

steam in. The eager listeners turn to you and you take them into the world of this absolutely hilarious or thrilling tale. As you relay the story, you picture it in your mind's eye, giving intricate detail, sometimes embellished and maybe at times completely exaggerated. The whole thing is delivered with a supreme flourish and your audience is agog, in the palm of your hand, and with you at the heart of the relayed events. This should also be the experience when delivering a Scripture reading.

As you familiarise yourself with the piece, picture the scene that you are setting, the characters, how they all feel and what is happening around them. You may think that, unless you actually say how the characters feel and what you imagine to be happening, it won't make any difference. This is not so – people can often read between the lines. If, as you read, you are picturing the story and enjoying telling it, as you would a personal recollection, the listener is drawn in.

I mention again the actors who think through their part rather than simply speak the words. In the texture of their voice and the look in their eyes you can see so much more than just what is being said. In a scene from one of my all-time favourite films, *One Flew Over the Cuckoo's Nest*, there is a shot of Jack Nicholson, silent and virtually motionless. The shot is held for what seems like ages, and without saying a single word he communicates to his audience exactly how he feels about his past, present and future situation. A brave film-making decision and a supreme example of acting. I'm not suggesting we do exactly this in our delivery of Scripture, but this lesson of storytelling can certainly be applied to a degree.

4. 'A cacophony of voices!' (Using multiple voices)

When we speak about multiple voices, it can mean one of two things: first, multiple voices adopted by a single reader, and second, multiple voices performed by a number of readers. I believe there is a place for both of these methods when communicating Scripture.

Using multiple voices will obviously not be everyone's strength and should only be attempted by someone who has the ability and confidence to carry it off. That's not to say they are better readers, or that it will necessarily make a better reading – it is just one possible style. The simple rule is that if you don't feel comfortable creating various character voices, don't do it, it's not essential. If it's not done well, it will actually do a lot more harm than good. I saw a wonderful actor create Hitler in a play recently and he didn't even attempt to use a German accent, but simply stuck with his own natural voice. I've no doubt he could have done a reasonable German accent, but he opted not to for his own artistic reasons, and in my opinion very wisely. The performance was so intense and thoughtful in other ways, that the audience were untroubled by a lack of ze German vords! In fact, some ham *'Allo 'Allo*-style attempt at an accent would certainly have detracted from his masterful performance.

On the other hand, there are countless classic examples of character voices which really add to performances. Simply put, it is down to a matter of style and preference. If you have the ability to create character voices, then experiment with them, without over-using them to the point of farce. If you can't do them, don't panic – it's not a big deal.

The second meaning of using multiple voices is by literally having multiple readers. In some of the selections in this book I have utilised this method, and it is also territory that has been well trodden before. It can be a very effective way of bringing the reading alive, in much the same style as a radio play, but simply using half a dozen people won't always equate to a powerful reading. The main risk is that if the readers don't do it very well, it actually compounds the problem you had with just one reader. I would suggest that a reading like this needs to be approached using the same criteria for preparation already discussed, of general understanding and rehearsal. Quite obviously it needs to be rehearsed in a similar way to a sketch, with all the readers together, getting used to their cues and bouncing effectively off one another. This will take a little more preparation time, but will certainly be worth the effort if it is done well.

5. 'Swing your stuff . . .' (Using movement)

Just because we are considering dramatising Bible readings, it does not mean that there has to be very much in the way of mime, movement or wild gesticulation. It is essential that we ensure first and foremost that the Scripture is communicated and we must not do anything to take away from that central objective. Nonetheless, using some physical movement in a dramatised reading, slight as it might be, is still very much worth considering.

Starting at the bottom end of the scale, sometimes you will notice that total stillness is the most powerful thing on stage. There's nothing more distracting than a reader endlessly fidgeting as if they've got an army of insects rampaging through their underwear! At other times, small movements and slight changes in position can help to focus attention or indicate a change of thought or emphasis. The Scriptures give rise to the full gamut of human emotions; these can often be referred to in verbal style, expression and basic movement. So if a movement adds to the narrative or emotional understanding of the piece, do it. If you think you're just moving about for the sheer sake of it, stop it. Stillness is an underrated stage position which is surprisingly hard to hold, but exceptionally effective. Think of Alan Bennett's *Talking Heads* monologues. The pieces are brilliantly written and when performed are powerful, yet there is hardly any movement required at all. Our attention is totally focused on the tale that is being told.

The movements I have suggested in the following selections are ones that I have found to work well, but the directions I give are not meant to be set in stone. If you have a different idea or feel uncomfortable doing what I suggest, you should ignore it. You need to believe in what you are doing in front of a congregation or audience. If you do it in a lacklustre fashion or feel a bit silly, this will certainly be noticed and in a very negative way. You need to feel confident in any piece of stagecraft you use; if you don't, it's best not to use it at all.

6. 'Play some funky tunes . . .' (Using music)

Music can be a brilliant communicator and tool for focusing particular emotions, if employed well. A few bars of well chosen music have the power to make us feel happy, downright depressed, Christmassy, summery and just about any other emotion you care to mention. Think also how many classic films have been defined by their brilliantly conceived soundtracks. The memorably searing cello in *Jaws* was expertly used to alert the audience that at any moment some innocent holiday swimmer was about to be savagely separated from one of their limbs. Or what about those creepy old black-and-white chillers, where the scene-setting music literally put the punters on the edge of their seats, nervously anticipating the next horrific sequence? Movie directors are very clever nowadays and even use the soundtrack to double bluff the audience. The music reaches a deafening crescendo and the crowd awaits the entrance of an axe-wielding maniac, only to discover that the culprit behind the creaky door is a stray cat or harmless barn owl. The result, however, is just as effective, sending the audience jumping six feet out of their seats, popcorn flying in all directions.

A great film will always have a great soundtrack, and not using music in a film now seems totally unimaginable. It is also great for use in live performance, or for our use here in dramatising Scripture. We can play a basic soundtrack and instantly set a tone or define a mood, focusing the listeners' attention. The danger, though, is that music can be so powerful that it takes away from the spoken word, or the reader will find it just about impossible to follow.

I can recall performing a monologue many years ago on National AIDS day, about the church's response to the causes and victims of this disease. As you can imagine, the piece was emotionally highly charged and, for a reason that eludes me now, I decided to open by walking very slowly from the rear of the hall with a backing tape of some tear-jerking classical music. (Okay, I know it sounds naff, but I was young and experimenting!) I can't remember exactly the piece of music I chose, but the immediate problem was that it was so powerful that quite a few people in the audience were sniffing and snivelling before I even opened my mouth. I like to think my performance was reasonably good, but I had made it so hard, giving myself such a tough act to follow. So however powerful and useful music can be for dramatic purposes, and I recommend it wholeheartedly, we must be aware that it has the potential to upstage us and should take this into account when preparing.

Using fairly brief excerpts at the top and tail of a reading is a good idea, giving the listeners a short moment to prepare and reflect. The issue of upstaging is most problematic if you use an extended chunk of music, so keep it short. Also, at certain times during a reading, you can quietly underplay some music through a section, choosing the moment very carefully so as not to overdo it and ruin the effect. Once we are aware of the dangers in allowing the music to upstage the reading, it is an easy task to use it powerfully in communicating the message.

7. 'Is it a bird? Is it a plane? No it's . . .' (Sound FX)

You may think that using sound effects may be a bit over the top for a Bible reading, but as with music, if it's used wisely and not overdone it can be very effective. Whether you are trying to create the sound of a particular environment, animal, location or whatever, sound effects can help you to create that mood. As with everything, there is a potential pitfall, and I would warn you against wandering too far down the path of outlandish comedy. Of course, if you are going for a laugh at a specific point, that's great, but you need to be aware that a sound effect can sometimes get a laugh at a totally inappropriate moment. Working this out is a matter of common sense.

For instance, if you are trying to communicate the raw emotion and despair of the prodigal son when he hits his all-time low eating pig slops, it is clearly not helpful to have someone making the noise of a pig wildly snorting all over the place. However, if you are trying to make a point about the sheer absurdity of this situation, a bit of controlled snorting could possibly be acceptable. We just need to be aware of what has the potential to cause laughter, and which elements of a story we are trying to communicate through the reading and teaching.

As for creating a sound effect to support your dramatising of Scripture, there are basically two methods you can use. First, any reasonably sized record shop or library should carry a stock of tapes and compact discs with a wide range of sounds. Each disc can carry well over a hundred sounds, so don't be concerned if lots of them appear to be totally unusable. If you only ever use twenty of the sounds, the disc will still be well worth the investment.

Alternatively, you can create the sounds vocally, either live on stage or by pre-recording them. This takes a bit more effort, but it is still reasonably easy to do, and it can have the added advantage of being made to sound exactly how you want it. For the texts used in this book, I have made certain suggestions for sound effects (FX), but as with all the directions given they are not set in stone and I would encourage individuals to think about trying some new and original ideas.

As well as using sound effects to set scenes, you can use basic props. These are great when performing drama, but with a dramatised reading it's probably not wise to go over the top. Nonetheless, a few well chosen and carefully placed items can prove useful on occasion. I have given a few ideas in the scripts of props you can use, but while you prepare you can have fun coming up with ideas of your own.

Here's a list of handy hints to summarise the main points from this chapter.

- **Understand it!** Yep, it's that one again. Remember, it is absolutely impossible to dramatise and communicate something to others without first understanding it yourself.
- **Speak clearly.** Make sure you pronounce each word clearly and don't mumble. When practising out loud, ask someone to listen in and tell you anything they didn't hear clearly or understand.
- **Vary tones.** Experiment using different tones depending on what you are communicating. Switching between softer and harder tones can help to give a clear indication of emotion.
- **To pause or not to pause?** With careful practice, ensure that you know the points in the text where you are required to pause. Well timed pauses can be very effective, but pausing at the wrong time can make you look very silly.
- **Tell the story.** While giving the reading, picture the scene and imagine telling the story. Although it does not add to the text in any direct way, using this technique will speak volumes in unspoken ways that your audience will pick up.

- **Character voices.** If reading a passage that has numerous characters, consider creating some suitable character voices to highlight the changes in dialogue. Only attempt this if you are confident about it and can sustain the voices throughout the reading.
- **Multiple readers.** Similar to the style of a radio play, consider the possible advantages of using multiple readers. If you do this, ensure all the readers understand the meaning of the text and take time to practise together. Some of the pieces in this collection have been scripted specifically for this purpose.
- **Movement and stillness.** Use any movements and changes in position wisely, not just as something to do. Using totally fidget-free stillness onstage is very powerful and suited to certain passages.
- **Music.** Think about how you might be able to use music to establish a particular mood or emotion. Always be aware that very powerful music has the ability to upstage the spoken word if it is overdone.
- **Sound effects (FX).** Either by buying a ready-made recording or by creating suitable sounds yourself, consider how you might add to the overall effect of the reading by using a variety of sound effects.
- **Props.** Can you use a few basic stage props to help communicate the text, without unnecessarily cluttering up the stage area?

Having examined the key pitfalls and looked at different techniques for dramatising the Scriptures, it's now about time to get reading!

Old Testament

1. The Beginning

IN A NUTSHELL

It seemed somewhat impossible, in a book of Bible readings, not to start with the creation as recorded in Genesis 1. I was tempted to miss it out, though, because if there is one passage that churches do already tend to dramatise, it is this.

The danger is that the passage is so well known that it can rather trip off the tongue with a careless familiarity, but it is so important that we consider the awesome questions it raises. They are central to our very existence. The opening words, 'In the beginning God created the heavens and the earth', contain in themselves much food for thought about the age-old questions of where we come from and where we are going. The text goes on to introduce the theme of God's creativity, his eternal state, his control and love, and also mankind's role and value to God.

The text can bring out the child in us, and I could regale many tales of hysterical and somewhat hammy dramatisations with children (and adults too!). The key for me with this reading is to keep it fairly straight and not succumb to the temptation of kitsch movements and farmyard animal impersonations. Note also the phrasing and structure, separating the story into neat sections, which, if communicated well, will help the listener to picture what is happening throughout.

Cast: NARRATOR, GOD.

Props: Sound FX: gentle wind; chirping birds; high-pitched note. Lighting. Banner or collage of sun, moon and stars.

THE READING

(*Darkness.* NARRATOR *stands in the centre,* GOD *is in an elevated position. Sound FX: gentle wind.*)

NARR: In the beginning God created the heavens and the earth. Now the earth was formless and empty, darkness was over the surface of the deep, and the Spirit of God was hovering over the waters. And God said,

GOD: Let there be light,

(*Lights suddenly go up.*)

NARR: and there was light. God saw that the light was good, and he separated the light from the darkness. God called the light 'day', and the darkness he called 'night'. And there was evening, and there was morning –

(*Sound FX: a single high-pitched note.*)

the first day. And God said,

GOD: Let there be an expanse between the waters to separate water from water.

NARR: So God made the expanse and separated the water under the expanse from the water above it. And it was so. God called the expanse 'sky'. And there was evening, and there was morning –

(*Sound FX: single high-pitched note.*)

the second day. And God said,

GOD: Let the water under the sky be gathered to one place, and let dry ground appear.

NARR: And it was so. God called the dry ground 'land', and the gathered waters he called 'seas'. And God saw that it was (*Emphasising*) good. Then God said,

GOD: Let the land produce vegetation: seed-bearing plants and trees on the land that bear fruit with seed in it, according to their various kinds.

NARR: And it was so. The land produced vegetation: plants bearing seed according to their kinds and trees bearing fruit with seed in it according to their kinds. And God saw that it was good. And there was evening, and there was morning –

(*Sound FX: single high-pitched note.*)

the third day. And God said,

GOD: Let there be lights in the expanse of the sky to separate the day from the night, and let them serve as signs to mark seasons and days and years, and let them be lights in the expanse of the sky to give light on the earth.

(*During this next paragraph, if it is possible unfurl a banner or collage depicting the sun, moon and stars. It needs to be of good quality or it will detract from the reading.*)

NARR: And it was so. God made two great lights – the greater light to govern the day and the lesser light to govern the night. He also made the stars. God set them in the expanse of the sky to give light on the earth, to govern the day and the night, and to separate light from darkness. And God saw that it was good. And there was evening, and there was morning –

(*Sound FX: single high-pitched note.*)

the fourth day. And God said,

GOD: Let the water teem with living creatures, and let birds fly above the earth across the expanse of the sky.

(*Sound FX: gentle chirping of birds.*)

NARR: So God created the great creatures of the sea and every living and moving thing with which the water teems, according to their kinds, and every winged bird according to its kind. And God saw that it was good. God blessed them and said,

GOD: Be fruitful and increase in number and fill the water in the seas, and let the birds increase on the earth.

NARR: And there was evening, and there was morning –

(*Sound FX: single high-pitched note.*)

the fifth day. And God said,

GOD: Let the land produce living creatures according to their kinds: livestock, creatures that move along the ground, and wild animals, each according to its kind.

NARR: And it was so. God made the wild animals according to their kinds, the livestock according to their kinds, and all the creatures that move along the ground according to their kinds. And God saw that it was good. Then God said,

GOD: Let us make man in our image, in our likeness, and let them rule over the fish of the sea and the birds of the air, over the livestock, over all the earth, and over all the creatures that move along the ground.

(*Background sound FX are raised higher, then stopped suddenly. Pause.*)

NARR: So God created man in his own image, in the image of God he created him; male and female he created them. God blessed them and said to them,

GOD: (*With genuine love*) Be fruitful and increase in number; fill the earth and subdue it. Rule over the fish of the sea and the birds of the air and over every living creature that moves on the ground.

I give you every seed-bearing plant on the face of the whole earth and every tree that has fruit with seed in it. They will be yours for food.

And to all the beasts of the earth and all the birds of the air and all the creatures that move on the ground – everything that has the breath of life in it – I give every green plant for food.

NARR: And it was so. God saw all that he had made, and it was (*Pause*) very good. And there was evening, and there was morning –

(*Sound FX: single high-pitched note.*)

the sixth day. Thus the heavens and the earth were completed in all their vast array.

(GOD *slowly begins to exit.*)

By the seventh day God had finished the work he had been doing; so on the seventh day he rested from all his work. And God blessed the seventh day and made it holy, because on it he rested from all the work of creating that he had done.

(*Sound FX brought up, lights fade into darkness.*)

NOTES

In this reading I have attempted to mix the more traditional communication of the creation story, using sound FX and visual aids, with a more powerful straight reading.

The reader of God's words should not speak in a celestial monotone, but with excitement and enthusiasm as he works on his treasured creation. As he sits on stage, he could perhaps use a large sketchbook or easel as a prop, indicating an artist at work.

GENESIS 3

2. Adam and Eve

IN A NUTSHELL

After the beautiful perfection of the creation, culminating in the design of man in Genesis 1, it only takes a couple of chapters before man blows it big style! As well as being a seminal scripture on the battle of good and evil and against temptation, in verse 15 we find the first pointer to Jesus Christ, and his victory over Satan.

Another of my personal favourite aspects of this story is the illustration of man futilely trying to hide his sin from God – something that I, of course, would never be so silly to try!

There are many ways to deliver this reading, but here I have used a radio play format, using a different reader for each character. It could be done with a single reader using a variety of voices, but the number of characters in a short space of time makes this a bit tricky.

Cast: NARRATOR, SERPENT, EVE, ADAM, GOD.

Props: Sound FX: sinister music. Bowl of fruit, including apples! Pieces of card depicting fig leaves. Two coats in a bag.

THE READING

(*Sinister music plays. Centre stage is a table with a big bowl of fruit. All readers walk on stage, freezing in a semicircle around the table. They break their freeze when they speak . . . music stops.*)

NARR:	Now the serpent
SERPENT:	(*Hisses*)
NARR:	was more crafty than any of the wild animals the Lord God had made. He said to the woman,
SERPENT:	(*Ultra smarmy*) Did God really say, 'You must not eat from any tree in the garden'?
EVE:	We may eat fruit from the trees in the garden, but God did say, 'You must not eat fruit from the tree that is in the middle of the garden, and you must not touch it, or you will die.'
SERPENT:	(*Mocking*) You will not surely die. For God knows that when you eat of it your eyes will be opened, and you will be like God, knowing good and (*Pause*) evil.
NARR:	When the woman saw that the fruit of the tree was good for food and pleasing to the eye, and also desirable for gaining wisdom, she took some and ate it.

(EVE *takes apple from bowl and has a bite.*)

> She also gave some to her husband, who was with her, and he ate it.

(EVE *throws an apple to* ADAM, *who also takes a bite.*)

> Then the eyes of both of them were opened, and they realised that they were naked; so they sewed fig leaves together and made coverings for themselves.

(*They hold prepared pieces of card in front of themselves depicting fig leaf coverings!*)

> Then the man and his wife heard the sound of the Lord God as he was walking in the garden

in the cool of the day, and thcy hid from the Lord God among the trees of the garden.

(They raise the cardboard coverings to hide faces.)

	But the Lord God called to the man,
GOD:	Where are you?
ADAM:	I heard you in the garden, and I was afraid because I was naked; so I hid.
GOD:	Who told you that you were naked? Have you eaten from the tree from which I commanded you not to eat?
ADAM:	*(Childishly passing the blame)* The woman you put here with me – she gave me some fruit from the tree, and I ate it.
GOD:	What is this you have done?
EVE:	*(Childishly passing the blame)* The serpent deceived me, and I ate.
NARR:	So the Lord God said to the serpent,
SERPENT:	*(Hisses)*
GOD:	Because you have done this, cursed are you above all the livestock and all the wild animals! You will crawl on your belly and you will eat dust all the days of your life.
	And I will put enmity between you and the woman, and between your offspring and hers; he will crush your head, and you will strike his heel. *(Indicate vocally or mime the victory in the crushing of the head)*
NARR:	To the woman he said,
GOD:	I will greatly increase your pains in childbearing; with pain you will give birth to children. Your desire will be for your husband, and he will rule over you.
NARR:	To Adam he said,

GOD: Because you listened to your wife and ate from the tree about which I commanded you, 'You must not eat of it,' cursed is the ground because of you; through painful toil you will eat of it all the days of your life.

It will produce thorns and thistles for you, and you will eat the plants of the field. By the sweat of your brow you will eat your food until you return to the ground, since from it you were taken; for dust you are and to dust you will return.

NARR: (*Short pause*) Adam named his wife Eve, because she would become the mother of all the living. The Lord God made garments of skin for Adam and his wife and clothed them.

(GOD *takes two coats from a bag and passes them to* ADAM *and* EVE.)

And the Lord God said,

GOD: (*Gravely*) The man has now become like one of us, knowing good and evil. He must not be allowed to reach out his hand and take also from the tree of life and eat, and live for ever.

NARR: (ADAM *and* EVE *exit as* NARRATOR *continues*) So the Lord God banished him from the Garden of Eden to work the ground from which he had been taken. After he drove the man out, he placed on the east side of the Garden of Eden cherubim and a flaming sword flashing back and forth to guard the way to the tree of life.

(*Music as all exit.*)

NOTES

I hope I am not out of place in saying that I believe there are elements of humour in this story which are fine to portray. We can be justified in laughing at our human frailty, demonstrated in Adam and Eve's ignorance of God's greatness and their childish behaviour.

However, it is important towards the end of the reading to communicate the gravity of their punishment and God's response to the fall of man. By painting the earlier verses with lighter tones, it can assist in bringing out the darker tones at the end.

3. Cain and Abel

IN A NUTSHELL

Genesis 4 records the famous story of Adam and Eve's sons, Cain and Abel. Cain was a farmer and Abel a shepherd, both typical occupations in the Middle East of today as well as in Bible times.

As well as documenting the first of many cruel murders in the Bible and the ramifications of that heinous crime, there is much to be learned about our attitude towards God and sin. In verse 5, why does God reject the offering of Cain, when he accepts Abel's in the previous verse? Maybe Cain had impure motives, or his offering was not up to standard. Whatever the reason, the lesson we learn in the story relates to our reactions to correction. Do we review and attempt to improve, get incredibly defensive, or become angry and bitter? As well as providing a truly shocking story, this reading has much to teach on reaction to correction and sin.

It is possible to do this as a solo reading, turning one way then another as each character speaks, but it can run into the danger of sounding like a Tommy Cooper routine. Here I have scripted it for two readers, with ONE predominantly reading the role of Cain.

Cast: ONE, TWO.

Props: None required.

THE READING

ONE: Adam lay with his wife Eve, and she became pregnant and gave birth to Cain. She said, 'With the help of the Lord I have brought forth a man.' Later she gave birth to his brother Abel. (*Look towards* TWO)

TWO: Now Abel kept flocks, and Cain worked the soil. In the course of time Cain brought some of the fruits of the soil as an offering to the Lord. (*Indicate that this was in some way a slovenly or unacceptable gift, given without due care*)

     But Abel brought fat portions from some of the firstborn of his flock. (*Indicate that this was a gift given with care and reverence*)

     The Lord looked with favour on Abel and his offering, but on Cain and his offering he did not look with favour. So Cain was very angry, and his face was downcast.

ONE: (*Downcast*) Then the Lord said to Cain, 'Why are you angry? Why is your face downcast? If you do what is right, will you not be accepted? But if you do not do what is right, sin is crouching at your door; it desires to have you, but you must master it.'

     (*Pause*) Now Cain said to his brother Abel, 'Let's go out to the field.' And while they were in the field, Cain attacked his brother Abel and killed him.

TWO: (*Pause*) Then the Lord said to Cain, 'Where is your brother Abel?'

ONE: (*Grumpily*) 'I don't know,' he replied. 'Am I my brother's keeper?'

TWO: The Lord said, 'What have you done? (*Pause*)

Listen! Your brother's blood cries out to me from the ground.

Now you are under a curse and driven from the ground, which opened its mouth to receive your brother's blood from your hand. When you work the ground, it will no longer yield its crops for you. You will be a restless wanderer on the earth.'

ONE: (*Pause*) Cain said to the Lord, 'My punishment is more than I can bear. Today you are driving me from the land, and I will be hidden from your presence; I will be a restless wanderer on the earth, and whoever finds me will kill me.'

TWO: But the Lord said to him, 'Not so; if anyone kills Cain, he will suffer vengeance seven times over.' Then the Lord put a mark on Cain so that no-one who found him would kill him.

So Cain went out from the Lord's presence and lived in the land of Nod, east of Eden.

NOTES

It may appear that I haven't added much in the way of dramatisation to this Scripture. Although the directions seem a bit sparse, if you take this reading steadily, giving it energy by really telling the story with emotion, it will come across very powerfully. Sometimes less is more!

GENESIS 22:1–14

4. Abraham and Isaac

IN A NUTSHELL

This is an incredibly challenging story, making us all re-evaluate and question our single-minded commitment to God. The obedience test that God sets Abraham seems in one sense unreal, even bordering on the cruel, but we must remember that God was not hoping to trip up Abraham, but rather to develop his character. When God sets us challenges, how do we respond? Negatively with a barrage of complaints, or positively with a desire to be changed?

Note also the parallels in this story with that of Christ on the cross. Here a ram is offered as a sacrifice in the place of Isaac; at Calvary Christ was offered as the sacrifice in place of us.

Cast: READER.

Props: Recording of discordant note or sound.

THE READING

READER: Some time later God tested Abraham. He said to him, 'Abraham!' 'Here I am,' he replied.

Then God said, 'Take your son, your only son, Isaac, whom you love, and go to the region of Moriah. Sacrifice him there as a burnt offering on one of the mountains I will tell you about.' (*Short pause for the gravity of this to sink in*)

Early the next morning Abraham got up and saddled his donkey. He took with him two of his servants and his son Isaac. When he had cut enough wood for the burnt offering, he set out for the place God had told him about.

On the third day Abraham looked up and saw the place in the distance. He said to his servants, (*Stuttering with trepidation*) 'Stay here with the donkey while I and the boy go over there. We will worship and then we will come back to you.' Abraham took the wood for the burnt offering and placed it on his son Isaac, and he himself carried the fire and the knife.

As the two of them went up together, Isaac spoke up and said to his father Abraham, 'Father?' 'Yes, my son?' Abraham replied. 'The fire and the wood are here,' Isaac said, 'but where is the lamb for the burnt offering?'

(*Pause, then moment of inspiration*) Abraham answered, 'God himself will provide the lamb for the burnt offering, my son.' And the two of them went on together.

When they reached the place God had told him about, Abraham built an altar there and arranged the wood on it. He bound his son Isaac and laid him on the altar, on top of the wood.

(*Single discordant note slowly builds to a high crescendo during this verse.*)

Then he reached out his hand and took the knife to slay his son.

(*Sudden silence.*)

But the angel of the Lord called out to him from heaven, 'Abraham! Abraham!' (*Quickly and very keenly*) 'Here I am,' he replied. 'Do not lay a hand on the boy. Do not do anything to him. Now I know that you fear God, because you have not withheld from me your son, your only son.' (*Pause*)

Abraham looked up and there in a thicket he saw a ram caught by its horns. He went over and took the ram and sacrificed it as a burnt offering instead of his son.

So Abraham called that place The Lord Will Provide. And to this day it is said, 'On the mountain of the Lord it will be provided.'

NOTES

In the NIV, this passage begins 'Some time later'. This begs the question, some time later than what? We should react to this by reading the preceding chapters to answer the question for ourselves, and then decide if it is necessary to put the reading into some form of verbal context for our listeners. Depending on your situation, it is not always necessary to do this, so I will leave that decision with you.

5. The Cupbearer and the Baker

IN A NUTSHELL

You could easily fill a whole book dramatising the extra-ordinary life of Joseph, but the single episode I have included here is the wonderfully visual tale of the cupbearer and baker.

Joseph's famous ability to interpret dreams is displayed here, one in a rather more positive way than the other. As Joseph matures, he loses his earlier tendency towards arrogance, and in this instance he is very open in deflecting the glory from himself to God as the source of the dreams' interpretations.

On being summarily forgotten by the surviving cupbearer, Joseph spends another two years festering in jail, but growing in faith, strength and character before his destined meeting with Pharaoh. The rest, as they say, is history . . .

Cast: NARRATOR, JOSEPH, CUPBEARER, BAKER.

Props: Seats, yo-yo.

THE READING

(*Lights up.* CUPBEARER *and* BAKER *seated centre stage looking worried.* BAKER *is playing with a yo-yo without success.* JOSEPH *is sleeping.*)

NARR: Some time later, the cupbearer and the baker of the king of Egypt offended their master, the king of Egypt. Pharaoh was angry with his two officials, the chief cupbearer and the chief baker, and put them in custody in the house of the captain of the guard, in the same prison where Joseph was confined. The captain of the guard assigned them to Joseph, and he attended them.

(JOSEPH *snores and* BAKER *throws yo-yo at him to wake him up.*)

After they had been in custody for some time, each of the two men – the cupbearer and the baker of the king of Egypt, who were being held in prison – had a dream the same night, and each dream had a meaning of its own.

When Joseph came to them the next morning, he saw that they were dejected. So he asked Pharaoh's officials who were in custody with him in his master's house,

JOSEPH: (*Rousing from sleep*) Why are your faces so sad today?

CUPBEARER: We both had dreams.

BAKER: But there is no-one to interpret them.

JOSEPH: (*Looking pleased*) Do not interpretations belong to God? Tell me your dreams.

NARR: So the chief cupbearer told Joseph his dream. He said to him,

CUPBEARER: (*Stands to animate his story*) In my dream I saw a vine in front of me, and on the vine were three branches. As soon as it budded, it blossomed, and its clusters ripened into grapes. Pharaoh's cup was in my hand, and I took the grapes, squeezed them into Pharaoh's cup and put the cup in his hand. (*Sits down looking confused by his dream*)

JOSEPH: (*Smiling confidently*) This is what it means. The
            three branches are three days. Within three
            days Pharaoh will lift up your head and restore
            you to your position, (JOSEPH *gets on chair and
            physically raises head*) and you will put
            Pharaoh's cup in his hand, just as you used to
            do when you were his cupbearer.

            (*Pause*) But when all goes well with you,
            remember me and show me kindness; mention
            me to Pharaoh and get me out of this prison.
            (*Hard done by*) For I was forcibly carried off
            from the land of the Hebrews, and even here I
            have done nothing to deserve being put in a
            dungeon.

NARR: When the chief baker saw that Joseph had
            given a favourable interpretation, he said to
            Joseph,

BAKER: (*Excited*) I too had a dream: (*Stands to animate
            story, copying* CUPBEARER) On my head were
            three baskets of bread. In the top basket were
            all kinds of baked goods for Pharaoh, but the
            birds were eating them out of the basket on my
            head.

JOSEPH: (*Pauses, then gravely*) This is what it means. The
            three baskets are three days. Within three days
            Pharaoh will lift off your head and hang you on
            a tree. And the birds will eat away your flesh.

(CUPBEARER *has look of frozen shock. As the truth becomes
clear he slowly resumes his seat.*)

NARR: Now the third day was Pharaoh's birthday, and
            he gave a feast for all his officials. He lifted up
            the heads of the chief cupbearer and the chief
            baker in the presence of his officials:

(CUPBEARER *and* BAKER *both stand.*)

> He restored the chief cupbearer to his position, so that he once again put the cup into Pharaoh's hand,

(CUPBEARER *exits looking very pleased with himself.*)

> but he hanged the chief baker, just as Joseph had said to them in his interpretation.

(BAKER *exits head hung low.*)

> The chief cupbearer, however, did not remember Joseph;

(JOSEPH, *alone, sits down, disappointed.*)

> he forgot him.

NOTES

Similarly to the reading in Genesis 22, this chapter opens with 'some time later', which should be researched to answer questions such as why Joseph was in prison. You may or may not wish to put this in a verbal context.

Although it is essential that we communicate the message of this text, there is certainly humour in the story, the baker being the butt of the joke. If we use that humour in a controlled way, it can greatly help with communicating the story.

6. The Ten Commandments

IN A NUTSHELL

God remains the same, not just throughout the Bible, but all through time and history. However, we do witness different aspects of his character – from his gentle and caring side, all the way through to his terrifying wrath. We should be under no illusion that in this chapter God is not messing around; he is giving instructions, not requests, and boy, do we ever need to listen up! Proof comes in verse 19 when the quaking crowd beg Moses to act as intermediary, scared that if God speaks to them they will surely die.

This piece, for one reader, should be delivered with the necessary gusto. If you read it nicely and politely, it weakens the desired impact. God is not gently suggesting we do these things, he is insisting on obedience, or the consequences will be frightening. I have put in some sound FX directions, but be aware that bursts of thunder and lightning can sometimes appear rather hammy and amateur.

Of course, simply obeying laws is not what true faith is about and can become legalistic. This chapter, however, is all about the law and we should not shrink from its teaching.

Cast: READER.

Props: Sound FX: thunder; wind.

THE READING

(*Sound FX: loud cracks of thunder. The reading can be underlined with the sound of wind and low rumbles, breaking into occasional claps of thunder. Delivery of the text should be stentorian.*)

READER: And God spoke all these words: I am the Lord your God, who brought you out of Egypt, out of the land of slavery.

(*Sound FX: thunder.*)

You shall have no other gods before me. You shall not make for yourself an idol in the form of anything in heaven above or on the earth beneath or in the waters below. You shall not bow down to them or worship them; for I, the Lord your God, am a jealous God, punishing the children for the sin of the fathers to the third and fourth generation of those who hate me, (*Lighter tones to indicate God's love*) but showing love to a thousand generations of those who love me and keep my commandments.

(*Sound FX: thunder.*)

You shall not misuse the name of the Lord your God, for the Lord will not hold anyone guiltless who misuses his name.

Remember the Sabbath day by keeping it holy. Six days you shall labour and do all your work, but the seventh day is a Sabbath to the Lord your God. On it you shall not do any work, neither you, nor your son or daughter, nor your manservant or maidservant, nor your animals, nor the alien within your gates.

For in six days the Lord made the heavens and the earth, the sea, and all that is in them, but he rested on the seventh day. Therefore the Lord blessed the Sabbath day and made it holy.

Honour your father and your mother, so that you may live long in the land the Lord your God is giving you.

(*Sound FX: thunder.*)

You shall not murder. (*Pause*) You shall not commit adultery. (*Pause*) You shall not steal. (*Pause*) You shall not give false testimony against your neighbour. (*Pause*)

You shall not covet your neighbour's house. You shall not covet your neighbour's wife, or his manservant or maidservant, his ox or donkey, or (*Emphasising*) anything that belongs to your neighbour.

(*Sound FX: thunder.*)

(*In this last section you revert to narration, not the voice of God, so alter your tone accordingly.*)

When the people saw the thunder and lightning and heard the trumpet and saw the mountain in smoke, they trembled with fear. They stayed at a distance and said to Moses, (*Fearfully*) 'Speak to us yourself and we will listen. But do not have God speak to us or we will die.'

Moses said to the people, (*Calming*) 'Do not be afraid. God has come to test you, so that the fear of God will be with you to keep you from sinning.'

The people remained at a distance, while Moses approached the thick darkness where God was.

(*Sound FX are heard for a few seconds, then slowly fade to silence.*)

NOTES

Because of the dramatic content of this chapter, it may seem strange not to make more of the passage physically. By creating semi-serious mimes and movements to these commands, we run the risk of lessening them or in some way sanitising the sins. If performing a sketch *based* on the Ten Commandments this is more acceptable, but it's probably unwise during an actual Scripture reading. Better to concentrate your efforts on creating a powerful and atmospheric straight delivery. Certainly, if working with children on this passage, getting them to act out the commands and then discussing them can greatly aid their understanding.

Some of the sentences in this passage are very long. Ensure that you read through it plenty of times and learn to avoid pausing in the wrong places.

7. Rahab and the Spies

IN A NUTSHELL

Joshua 2 gives us a great cloak-and-dagger story, and offers real encouragement for anyone who thinks they're not holy enough to become a Christian! The prostitute Rahab certainly had a chequered past, but that did not stop her faith in God's ability.

As well as reading around Joshua 2, if you leap on to chapter 6 you can read what happened to Rahab and her family when the walls of Jericho fell. So incredible is God's forgiveness that she is mentioned as one of the heroes of faith in Hebrews 11. When reading, imagine Rahab's fearless nature and the selfless sacrifice she was prepared to make for what, in essence, were two strangers.

Rather than split the reading into numerous parts, I have scripted this one for two readers, one playing Rahab, the other narrating and covering the other small parts.

Cast: RAHAB, NARRATOR.

Props: Red cord.

THE READING

NARR: Then Joshua son of Nun secretly sent two spies from Shittim. 'Go, look over the land,' he said, 'especially Jericho.' So they went and entered the house of a prostitute named Rahab and stayed there.

The king of Jericho was told, 'Look! Some of the Israelites have come here tonight to spy out the land.' So the king of Jericho sent this message to Rahab:

(*Commanding*) 'Bring out the men who came to you and entered your house, because they have come to spy out the whole land.'

But the woman had taken the two men and hidden them. She said,

RAHAB: (*Innocently*) Yes, the men came to me, but I did not know where they had come from. At dusk, when it was time to close the city gate, the men left. I don't know which way they went. Go after them quickly. You may catch up with them.

(*Pause, then aside to audience*) But she had taken them up to the roof and hidden them under the stalks of flax she had laid out on the roof.

NARR: So the men set out in pursuit of the spies on the road that leads to the fords of the Jordan, and as soon as the pursuers had gone out, the gate was shut.

Before the spies lay down for the night, she went up on the roof and said to them,

RAHAB: (*Impressed and excited at God's power*) I know that the Lord has given this land to you and that a great fear of you has fallen on us, so that all who live in this country are melting in fear because of you. We have heard how the Lord dried up the water of the Red Sea for you when you came out of Egypt, and what you did to Sihon and Og, the two kings of the Amorites east of the Jordan, whom you completely destroyed.

When we heard of it, our hearts sank and everyone's courage failed because of you, for the Lord your God is God in heaven above and on the earth below. (*Pleading her case*) Now then, please swear to me by the Lord that you will show kindness to my family, because I have shown kindness to you.

Give me a sure sign that you will spare the lives of my father and mother, my brothers and sisters, and all who belong to them, and that you will save us from death.

NARR: 'Our lives for your lives!' the men assured her. 'If you don't tell what we are doing, we will treat you kindly and faithfully when the Lord gives us the land.'

So she let them down by a rope through the window, for the house she lived in was part of the city wall. Now she had said to them,

RAHAB: Go to the hills so that the pursuers will not find you. Hide yourselves there three days until they return, and then go on your way.

NARR: The men said to her, 'This oath you made us swear will not be binding on us unless, when we enter the land, you have tied this scarlet cord (*Produces a scarlet cord*) in the window through which you let us down, and unless you have brought your father and mother, your brothers and all your family into your house.

'If anyone goes outside your house into the street, his blood will be on his own head; we will not be responsible. (*Pause*) As for anyone who is in the house with you, his blood will be on our head if a hand is laid on him.

(*Final stern warning*) 'But if you tell what we

	are doing, we will be released from the oath you made us swear.'
RAHAB:	Agreed. Let it be as you say.
NARR:	So she sent them away and they departed. And she tied the scarlet cord in the window.

(RAHAB *ties cord to lectern or similar, then exits.*)

When they left, they went into the hills and stayed there three days, until the pursuers had searched all along the road and returned without finding them.

Then the two men started back. They went down out of the hills, forded the river and came to Joshua son of Nun and told him everything that had happened to them. They said to Joshua, 'The Lord has surely given the whole land into our hands; all the people are melting in fear because of us.'

NOTES

If done well, this can be a very atmospheric reading, especially the lovely plea by Rahab in verses 9–13. As given in the directions, an optional extra is to use a red cord, to be tied to an appropriate place. This is a useful visual aid and could be further used or referred to during a sermon, with the obvious parallel of the saving quality of Christ's blood.

8. Samson and Delilah

IN A NUTSHELL

The story of Samson is told in Judges 13–16, and for this first selection I have chosen the great story of his doomed affair with Delilah. It is a wonderful tale, laced with black humour as we recognise some classic human foibles, but carrying an overall dark message of love and betrayal.

We can easily categorise Samson as a lumbering fool, not immediately catching on to Delilah's lies, but if we're honest it's very easy for us to be deceived by lust, blinded by a desire we so want to believe. Samson was a mighty man of God (read the full story of his feats), but he was misguided to forget his calling and ultimately not even realise that God's strength had left him. This had horrible consequences and is an important lesson for us to learn and communicate.

The reading is split into three parts (Samson, Delilah and the narrator) offering an opportunity to display the male/female psychology of Delilah's deceit.

Cast: SAMSON, DELILAH, NARRATOR.

Props: Sound FX: introductory music for Samson; romantic music. 'Heavy' weight. Moneybag.

THE READING

(NARRATOR *stands at side of stage. Heroic music plays as* SAMSON *enters hauling some heavy weight. He sits centre stage looking mighty.*)

NARR: Some time later, Samson fell in love with a
                woman in the Valley of Sorek whose name was
                Delilah.

(DELILAH *enters seductively to a short blast of romantic music.
She stands by* NARRATOR, SAMSON *looks on keenly.*)

                The rulers of the Philistines went to her and
                said, (*Conspiratorially whispering to* DELILAH)
                'See if you can lure him into showing you the
                secret of his great strength and how we can
                overpower him so that we may tie him up and
                subdue him. Each one of us will give you eleven
                hundred shekels of silver.'

(DELILAH *nods agreement and goes over to sit with* SAMSON,
flirting.)

DELILAH: (*To* SAMSON) Tell me the secret of your great
                strength and how you can be tied up and
                subdued.
SAMSON: If anyone ties me with seven fresh thongs that
                have not been dried, I'll become as weak as any
                other man.
DELILAH: (*Directed to audience*) Then the rulers of the
                Philistines brought her seven fresh thongs that
                had not been dried, and she tied him with them.
                With men hidden in the room, she called to
                him, (*Like a very bad actress*) 'Samson, the
                Philistines are upon you!'
NARR: (*Disappointed*) But he snapped the thongs as
                easily as a piece of string snaps when it comes
                close to a flame. So the secret of his strength
                was not discovered. Then Delilah said to
                Samson,

DELILAH: (*Sulkily*) You have made a fool of me; you lied to me. Come now, tell me how you can be tied.

SAMSON: If anyone ties me securely with new ropes that have never been used, I'll become as weak as any other man.

DELILAH: (*Once more to audience*) So Delilah took new ropes and tied him with them. Then, with men hidden in the room, she called to him, (*As before*) 'Samson, the Philistines are upon you!'

NARR: (*Pause*) But he snapped the ropes off his arms as if they were threads. Delilah then said to Samson,

DELILAH: (*Huffy*) Until now, you have been making a fool of me and lying to me. (*Pleading*) Tell me how you can be tied.

SAMSON: If you weave the seven braids of my head into the fabric on the loom and tighten it with the pin, I'll become as weak as any other man.

DELILAH: (*To audience, but visibly getting fed up*) So while he was sleeping, Delilah took the seven braids of his head, wove them into the fabric and tightened it with the pin. Again she called to him, 'Samson, the Philistines are upon you!'

NARR: (*Totally dejected*) He awoke from his sleep and pulled up the pin and the loom, with the fabric. Then she said to him,

DELILAH: (*Fakes upset, with wobbly bottom lip*) How can you say, 'I love you,' when you won't confide in me? (*Gets angry*) This is the third time you have made a fool of me and haven't told me the secret of your great strength.

SAMSON: (*To audience*) With such nagging she prodded him day after day until he was tired to death. So he told her everything. (*To* DELILAH) No razor has ever been used on my head, because I have been a Nazirite set apart to God since birth. If my head were shaved, my strength would leave me, and I would become as weak as any other man.

NARR: When Delilah saw that he had told her everything, she sent word to the rulers of the Philistines,

DELILAH: Come back once more; he has told me everything.

NARR: So the rulers of the Philistines returned with the silver in their hands. (NARRATOR *throws moneybag to* DELILAH)

DELILAH: (*Lays* SAMSON *in her lap*) Having put him to sleep on her lap, she called a man to shave off the seven braids of his hair, and so began to subdue him. And his strength left him. Then she called, (*Quietly*) 'Samson, the Philistines are upon you!'

SAMSON: (*Slowly sits up*) He awoke from his sleep and thought, 'I'll go out as before and shake myself free.' But he did not know that the Lord had left him.

NARR: (*Gravely*) Then the Philistines seized him, gouged out his eyes and took him down to Gaza. Binding him with bronze shackles, they set him to grinding in the prison. But the hair on his head began to grow again after it had been shaved.

(*During the last speech* DELILAH *slowly leads* SAMSON *off stage.*)

NOTES

Although in this scripted version we are in effect acting out the story onstage, we are letting the text do the work apart from basic movements. Physically making a scrappy effort at miming or actually tying Samson up four times will get a tad boring. By allowing Delilah to speak words as an aside to the audience as she tells the story picturing what she describes, the audience is carried along.

You may get some laughs in the first part of this text, which I believe is justified. However, from verse 17 the mood should be dramatically changed as we see the consequences of Samson's choices.

9. Death of Samson

IN A NUTSHELL

When collating the readings for this book, I asked many learned people from a wide range of church backgrounds to make suggestions for key passages. This, to my surprise, was one of the most popular choices. I had always planned to include the story of Samson and Delilah, but coupled with it is the story of Samson's destruction of the temple and his death. This is the culmination of Samson's story and paints a very moving picture of a great man brought to his knees, but given the strength to perform a final, seemingly impossible, feat.

It is very easy to do a stage performance of this reading. I have split this into four speaking roles, though you will also need some non-speaking performers: the servant, and a few people to form a crowd.

Cast: NARRATOR, SAMSON, ONE, TWO. (*Plus* SERVANT *and* CROWD *as non-speaking parts.*)

Props: Sound FX: trumpet music; sound of collapsing building.

THE READING

(*Music: trumpet salute or similar to indicate music of a court or temple.* CROWD *enter and take positions scattered around stage, depending on numbers.*)

NARR: Now the rulers of the Philistines assembled to offer a great sacrifice to Dagon their god and to celebrate, saying, 'Our god has delivered Samson, our enemy, into our hands.' When the people saw him, they praised their god, saying,

ONE: (*Vitriolic*) Our god has delivered our enemy into our hands, the one who laid waste our land and multiplied our slain.

(CROWD *give vocal agreement.*)

NARR: While they were in high spirits, they shouted,

TWO: Bring out Samson to entertain us.

NARR: So they called Samson out of the prison, and he performed for them.

(SAMSON *is led on by* SERVANT *to general jeering, clapping and merriment of the* CROWD. *They do this loudly for a few seconds, then continue in slow-motion mime, laughing, pointing and talking among themselves.*)

           When they stood him among the pillars, Samson said to the servant who held his hand,

SAMSON: (*Quietly*) Put me where I can feel the pillars that support the temple, so that I may lean against them.

(SERVANT *moves the blind* SAMSON *to front and centre stage.*)

NARR: Now the temple was crowded with men and women; all of the rulers of the Philistines were there, and on the roof were about three thousand men and women watching Samson perform. Then Samson prayed to the Lord,

SAMSON: (*Quietly and precisely*) O Sovereign Lord,

remember me. O God, please strengthen me just once more, and let me with one blow get revenge on the Philistines for my two eyes.

NARR: Then Samson reached towards the two central pillars on which the temple stood. Bracing himself against them, his right hand on the one and his left hand on the other, Samson said,

SAMSON: (*Loudly*) Let me die with the Philistines!

NARR: Then he pushed with all his might, and down came the temple on the rulers and all the people in it.

(SAMSON *extends his arms sideways, miming pushing pillars. Sound FX: deafening destruction of building.* CROWD *look up in horror and with choreographed slow movements curl bodies and drop to knees. As the noise fades and all are on their knees,* SAMSON *remains standing and smiling heavenwards.*)

Thus he killed many more when he died than while he lived.

(SAMSON *also slowly drops to his knees.*)

NOTES

Having a crowd on stage can be highly effective, but it can also be a real liability. Sometimes a non-speaking role can be harder than a main one, as it is more difficult to be believable. The key thing is to concentrate on what your character would be doing (if anything at all) or thinking, and show this without going totally over the top. If you're standing there madly waving your arms or pulling faces, you will naturally remove attention from the text; however, if you just stand there blankly, unaware of what's going on or why you're actually onstage in the first place, you will also look totally out of place.

Observe people having a conversation at a distance and make a note of the movements they make. On the whole they are small movements – a slight shake of the head, a shrug of the shoulders or a gesture with the hand is usually about as animated as it gets. People rarely rock back and forth with laughter; they more often smile and slightly tip their heads. These movements, once observed, are easily imitated.

For the crowd scene in this text, I have suggested a verbal explosion when Samson is brought in, almost immediately changing to mime and movement. In this instance I believe that constant shrieks from the crowd ensemble would be intrusive (although that is not always necessarily the case) and a cacophony of 'aagghhs' as the temple falls would sound a bit cheesy and undermine the power of the text. Better to leave a bit more to the imagination and the powerful image of Samson victorious in death.

RUTH 3

10. Ruth and Boaz

IN A NUTSHELL

It may only have four chapters, but Ruth is one of the most inspiring books in the Old Testament. It tells the story of an amazing woman and great hero of faith. In this chapter we also discover some interesting culture of the time regarding marriage rites and the kinsman-redeemer. Spending some time researching this in a commentary is well worthwhile, but basically a kinsman-redeemer was a relative who voluntarily agreed to take responsibility for a woman who had been widowed. The sequence in verses 4–6 at the threshing-floor displays an Israelite custom, indicating Ruth's request for Boaz to act as her kinsman-redeemer.

Originally this story was not meant to be funny, but with the passage of time and huge changes in culture, it is quite amusing to think of someone making a move on a potential partner by uncovering their feet! This, however, displays an innocent kind of humour and we must not turn it into some highly farcical situation, which would be easy to do. Of course we do things differently now, but at the time this practice was totally acceptable and even romantic!

It is worth reading the whole book to get it into context for yourself and, depending on the sermon, it might be worth putting it into some form of contextual setting for the listeners. Check this with whoever is preaching, as they may go into the cultural practices in their planned message. I've scripted this without using a narrator, simply the three characters, each telling their particular parts of the story.

Cast: NAOMI, RUTH, BOAZ.

Props: Sound FX: sudden noise.

THE READING

(BOAZ *is stage left, working on his hands and knees.* NAOMI *is seated stage right, with* RUTH *kneeling by her side. During* NAOMI*'s first speech, try and communicate the real, loving relationship between mother and daughter-in-law. Also during this section* BOAZ *should mime working, then settling back with a drink. By the end of* NAOMI*'s speech, he should be just starting to drink.*)

NAOMI: One day Naomi her mother-in-law (*Holds hand to chest indicating that it's her*) said to her, 'My daughter, should I not try to find a home for you, where you will be well provided for? Is not Boaz, with whose servant girls you have been, a kinsman of ours?

(*As if sharing a secret plan with* RUTH) 'Tonight he will be winnowing barley on the threshing-floor. Wash and perfume yourself, and put on your best clothes. Then go down to the threshing-floor, but don't let him know you are there until he has finished eating and drinking.

'When he lies down, note the place where he is lying. Then go and uncover his feet and lie down. (*Knowingly*) He will tell you what to do.'

RUTH: 'I will do whatever you say,' Ruth answered. So she went down to the threshing-floor and did everything her mother-in-law told her to do.

(RUTH *slowly moves to the other side of the stage.*)

BOAZ: When Boaz had finished eating and drinking and was in good spirits, he went over to lie down at the far end of the grain pile. (*He does so as he speaks, ending up lying on the floor*)

RUTH: Ruth approached quietly, uncovered his feet and lay down. (*She does*)

BOAZ: (*Pause*) In the middle of the night something startled the man,

(*Sound FX: any noise which serves to suddenly wake* BOAZ.)

and he turned and discovered a woman lying at his feet. (*Confused*) Who are you?

RUTH: I am your servant Ruth. Spread the corner of your garment over me, since you are a kinsman-redeemer.

BOAZ: (*Pause, he smiles in realisation of her kindness and situation*) The Lord bless you, my daughter. (*Spreads cover over* RUTH) This kindness is greater than that which you showed earlier: You have not run after the younger men, whether rich or poor.

And now, my daughter, don't be afraid. I will do for you all you ask. All my fellow townsmen know that you are a woman of noble character. Although it is true that I am near of kin, there is a kinsman-redeemer nearer than I.

Stay here for the night, and in the morning if he wants to redeem, good; let him redeem. But if he is not willing, as surely as the Lord lives I will do it. Lie here until morning.

RUTH: (*To audience*) So she lay at his feet until morning, but got up before anyone could be recognised.

BOAZ: (*To* RUTH) Don't let it be known that a woman

came to the threshing-floor. Bring me the shawl you are wearing and hold it out. (*She does*)

(*To audience*) When she did so, he poured into it six measures of barley and put it on her. (*Loosely mime this action*) Then he went back to town.

(BOAZ *exits,* RUTH *returns to* NAOMI, *who has been quietly watching the events.*)

NAOMI: (*Pleased at* RUTH's *return*) How did it go, my daughter? (*To audience*) Then she told me everything Boaz had done for her.

RUTH: (*Excited*) He gave me these six measures of barley, saying, 'Don't go back to your mother-in-law empty-handed.'

NAOMI: Wait, my daughter, until you find out what happens. For the man will not rest until the matter is settled today.

NOTE

For this reading you can communicate the bedcover and shawl by using either actual props (ie plain dust sheets) or a simple mime.

11. David and Goliath

IN A NUTSHELL

What a great and classic story this one is! It's a bit of a long one, but if read well it will keep the listeners' attention. Read around the chapter to familiarise yourself with the Israel/Philistine situation and the turmoils of David. Here we see him fresh-faced and innocent, maybe prone to a degree of complacency, but on the verge of one of his greatest triumphs. At about ten feet tall, Goliath had an obvious physical advantage over David, but this story teaches us a truth about allowing God to help us overcome our giants.

I've scripted this in radio play format, with a group of readers, and doubling up on parts is possible if required. As well as telling the story, aim to understand and communicate the characters and emotions displayed.

Cast: NARRATOR, GOLIATH, DAVID, JESSE, ELIAB, CROWD ENSEMBLE, including SHIELD-BEARER.

Props: Sound FX: opening music; crowing cockerel. Shield. Two cuddly sheep. Tunic, helmet and sword. Five stones and pouch.

THE READING

(*Play some opening music suitable for a call to battle – maybe something like Queen's, 'We Will Rock You!' The* NARRATOR, *as a TV reporter, is at side of stage.* CROWD ENSEMBLE *is lined up at back of stage.*)

NARR: (*As news reporter*) A champion named Goliath, who was from Gath, came out of the Philistine camp.

(GOLIATH *enters with* CROWD ENSEMBLE. SHIELD-BEARER *enters on knees in front of him holding shield of armour.*)

He was over nine feet tall. He had a bronze helmet on his head and wore a coat of scale armour of bronze weighing five thousand shekels; on his legs he wore bronze greaves, and a bronze javelin was slung on his back. His spear shaft was like a weaver's rod, and its iron point weighed six hundred shekels. His shield-bearer went ahead of him. Goliath stood and shouted to the ranks of Israel,

GOLIATH: Why do you come out and line up for battle? Am I not a Philistine, and are you not the servants of Saul? Choose a man and have him come down to me. If he is able to fight and kill me, we will become your subjects; but if I overcome him and kill him, you will become our subjects and serve us. This day I defy the ranks of Israel!

(CROWD *cheer*.)

Give me a man and let us fight each other.

NARR: On hearing the Philistine's words, Saul and all the Israelites were dismayed and terrified.

(*Cast freeze, slight pause.* DAVID *steps forward either holding or pulling a couple of sheep. Cuddly toys will suffice if the real thing is not available!*)

Now David was the son of an Ephrathite named Jesse, who was from Bethlehem in

Judah. Jesse had eight sons, and in Saul's time he was old and well advanced in years. Jesse's three oldest sons had followed Saul to the war: The firstborn was Eliab; the second Abinadab; and the third Shammah. David was the youngest. The three oldest followed Saul, but David went back and forth from Saul to tend his father's sheep at Bethlehem.

For forty days the Philistine came forward every morning and evening and took his stand. Now Jesse said to his son David,

JESSE: Take this ephah of roasted grain and these ten loaves of bread for your brothers and hurry to their camp. Take along these ten cheeses to the commander of their unit. See how your brothers are and bring back some assurance from them. They are with Saul and all the men of Israel in the Valley of Elah, fighting against the Philistines.

(*Sound FX: Cock a doodle doo!*)

NARR: Early in the morning David left the flock with a shepherd, loaded up and set out, as Jesse had directed. He reached the camp as the army was going out to its battle positions, shouting the war cry.

(CROWD *cry out, which makes* DAVID *jump.*)

Israel and the Philistines were drawing up their lines facing each other. David left his things with the keeper of supplies, ran to the battle lines and greeted his brothers.

(DAVID *joins* CROWD ENSEMBLE.)

As he was talking with them, Goliath, the Philistine champion from Gath, stepped out from his lines and shouted his usual defiance, and David heard it. When the Israelites saw the man, they all ran from him in great fear. Now the Israelites had been saying,

CROWD: (*Any one, or mixture, in an effort to tempt* DAVID) Do you see how this man keeps coming out? He comes out to defy Israel. The king will give great wealth to the man who kills him. He will also give him his daughter in marriage and will exempt his father's family from taxes in Israel.

NARR: David asked the men standing near him,

DAVID: (*Showing subdued interest*) What will be done for the man who kills this Philistine and removes this disgrace from Israel? Who is this uncircumcised Philistine that he should defy the armies of the living God?

NARR: They repeated to him what they had been saying and told him, 'This is what will be done for the man who kills him.' When Eliab, David's oldest brother, heard him speaking with the men, he burned with anger at him and asked,

ELIAB: (*Patronising*) Why have you come down here? And with whom did you leave those few sheep in the desert? I know how conceited you are and how wicked your heart is; you came down only to watch the battle.

DAVID: (*Innocently*) Now what have I done? Can't I even speak?

NARR: He then turned away to someone else and brought up the same matter, and the men answered him as before. What David said was overheard and reported to Saul, and Saul sent for him. David said to Saul,

(DAVID *can't see* SAUL. SAUL *steps forward and taps him on shoulder.*)

DAVID: (*Confidently*) Let no-one lose heart on account of this Philistine; your servant will go and fight him.

SAUL: (*Stunned pause, then smiling*) You are not able to go out against this Philistine and fight him; you are only a boy, and he has been a fighting man from his youth.

DAVID: Your servant has been keeping his father's sheep. When a lion or a bear came and carried off a sheep from the flock, I went after it, struck it and rescued the sheep from its mouth. When it turned on me, I seized it by its hair, struck it and killed it.

Your servant has killed both the lion and the bear; this uncircumcised Philistine will be like one of them, because he has defied the armies of the living God. The Lord who delivered me from the paw of the lion and the paw of the bear will deliver me from the hand of this Philistine.

SAUL: (*Pause for thought*) Go, and the Lord be with you.

NARR: Then Saul dressed David in his own tunic. He put a coat of armour on him and a bronze helmet on his head. David fastened on his sword over the tunic and tried walking around, because he was not used to them.

(*While* NARRATOR *speaks,* SAUL *dresses* DAVID *in token props — the full list is not necessary.* DAVID *tries to walk, unsuccessfully.*)

DAVID: (*Irritated*) I cannot go in these, because I am not used to them.

NARR: So he took them off. Then he took his staff in
             his hand, chose five smooth stones from the
             stream,

(DAVID *picks up five stones from front of stage, which have been
in position from beginning.*)

             put them in the pouch of his shepherd's bag
             and, with his sling in his hand, approached the
             Philistine.

(GOLIATH *and* SHIELD-BEARER *step forward to face* DAVID.)

             Meanwhile, the Philistine, with his shield-
             bearer in front of him, kept coming closer to
             David. He looked David over and saw that he
             was only a boy, ruddy and handsome, and he
             despised him. He said to David,

GOLIATH: Am I a dog, that you come at me with sticks?

(CROWD *cheer* GOLIATH *and jeer at* DAVID.)

NARR: And the Philistine cursed David by his gods.

GOLIATH: Come here, and I'll give your flesh to the birds
             of the air and the beasts of the field!

DAVID: (*Powerfully and with passion*) You come against
             me with sword and spear and javelin, but I
             come against you in the name of the Lord
             Almighty, the God of the armies of Israel,
             whom you have defied.
                 This day the Lord will hand you over to me,
             and I'll strike you down and cut off your head.
             Today I will give the carcasses of the Philistine
             army to the birds of the air and the beasts of

the earth, and the whole world will know that
there is a God in Israel.

All those gathered here will know that it is
not by sword or spear that the Lord saves; for
the battle is the Lord's, and he will give all of
you into our hands.

(*During* DAVID's *speech the cast are still and silent. At the
end there is a moment's pause before the* NARRATOR *continues.*)

NARR: As the Philistine moved closer to attack him,
David ran quickly towards the battle line to
meet him. Reaching into his bag and taking out
a stone, he slung it and struck the Philistine on
the forehead.

(DAVID *takes a stone and mimes throwing action, a* MEMBER OF
THE ENSEMBLE *takes the stone and walks slowly, arm raised, to*
GOLIATH, *where he touches it on his head.* GOLIATH *falls and the*
MEMBER OF THE ENSEMBLE *resumes his position.*)

The stone sank into his forehead, and he fell
face down on the ground.

(*There is a stunned pause, then the* CROWD *cheer.* GOLIATH's
SHIELD-BEARER *slopes off to the side.*)

So David triumphed over the Philistine with
a sling and a stone; without a sword in his
hand he struck down the Philistine and killed
him.

(*Opening music plays as* DAVID *exits acknowledging the*
CROWD's *general merriment.*)

NOTES

Due to the length of this piece and the number of characters, it's probably not wise to attempt to perform each described action, or the whole thing could look rather clumsy. Put the narrator/TV reporter to the side of the stage, David and Goliath at front of stage and the other smaller parts around them as an ensemble at the back. Restrict the actions to David and Goliath, with the ensemble at the back simply reading their parts and creating sound effects. When David is talking with members of the ensemble, they can simply step forward.

When we speak of an ensemble, it basically means a group of performers who can switch between a variety of roles. They can be cheering Goliath one minute, and the next can act as the voice of Saul. It is a common and acceptable form of performance, which cuts down required numbers and should not confuse the audience.

This story will communicate well in this format and will be both powerful and amusing in places. Ensure that David's speech in verses 45–47 is well rehearsed and given due importance.

12. David and Nathan

IN A NUTSHELL

In contrast to David's victory over Goliath, this reading shows the other side of the flawed biblical giant. Flick back a few chapters from this passage and you will read David's heartfelt prayer, the lists of victories – and then, in chapter 11, the story of his lust, which leads to murder. Imagine how he must have felt, falling from such lofty heights to base, immoral behaviour. Nathan rebukes David and confronts him with the terrible truth of his sin. Imagine the guts it must have taken to confront a king with his wrongdoing! David is so mired in his sin that he can't even recognise himself in Nathan's story, until he's told, 'You are the man.'

I've scripted this for two readers, relying on the power of the dialogue and the emotions it conjures up. There is little movement; the two characters simply sit facing each other. Since the story relies on the narrative, the readers should ensure they know the verses very well, enabling them to look up and communicate the meaning more powerfully.

Cast: NATHAN, DAVID.

Props: Sound FX: mournful music. Two chairs.

THE READING

(*Mournful music. Two chairs face each other.* DAVID *is seated on one in deep thought.*)

NATHAN: (*Enters*) The Lord sent Nathan to David. (*Sits opposite* DAVID) When he came to him, he said,

(*Music suddenly stops and* DAVID *looks up.*)

(*Storytelling mode*) There were two men in a certain town, one rich and the other poor. The rich man had a very large number of sheep and cattle, but the poor man had nothing except one little ewe lamb that he had bought.

He raised it, and it grew up with him and his children. It shared his food, drank from his cup and even slept in his arms. It was like a daughter to him.

Now a traveller came to the rich man, but the rich man refrained from taking one of his own sheep or cattle to prepare a meal for the traveller who had come to him. (*With obvious disdain*) Instead, he took the ewe lamb that belonged to the poor man and prepared it for the one who had come to him.

DAVID: David burned with anger against the man and said to Nathan, (*Angrily*) As surely as the Lord lives, the man who did this deserves to die! (*Judging*) He must pay for that lamb four times over, because he did such a thing and had no pity.

NATHAN: Then Nathan said to David, (*Pause*) You are the man! This is what the Lord, the God of Israel, says:

(*Disappointed*) 'I anointed you king over Israel, and I delivered you from the hand of Saul. I gave your master's house to you, and your master's wives into your arms. I gave you the house of Israel and Judah. And if all this had been too little, I would have given you even more.

'Why did you despise the word of the Lord by doing what is evil in his eyes? (*Accusing*) You struck down Uriah the Hittite with the sword and took his wife to be your own.

(DAVID *hangs his head, knowing he is discovered.*)

'You killed him with the sword of the Ammonites. Now, therefore, the sword shall never depart from your house, because you despised me and took the wife of Uriah the Hittite to be your own.'

This is what the Lord says: 'Out of your own household I am going to bring calamity upon you. Before your very eyes I will take your wives and give them to one who is close to you, and he will lie with your wives in broad daylight. You did it in secret, but I will do this thing in broad daylight before all Israel.'

DAVID: (*Pause*) I have sinned against the Lord.
NATHAN: The Lord has taken away your sin. You are not going to die. But because by doing this you have made the enemies of the Lord show utter contempt, the son born to you will die.

(NATHAN *and* DAVID *look directly at each other, music plays quietly as they exit opposite sides.*)

NOTES

For the reader playing Nathan, the first half should be told as a story, lulling David into a false sense of security. From the point when he says, 'You are the man,' in verse 7, the tone should change as he delivers the truth of David's sin and its grave consequences. The lines should not be rushed, but should be completely clear.

For the reader playing David, he will need to react to Nathan's words. His righteous indignation in verses 5 and 6 is pronounced because of his own guilty conscience, and this can be communicated silently. When Nathan is reading God's judgement, the reader should imagine the kind of emotions David experiences and communicate this with slight facial and bodily gestures.

13. Solomon's Wise Ruling

IN A NUTSHELL

Turning now to the great story of King Solomon, I have chosen one of the more famous episodes, which also lends itself perfectly to a dramatic telling.

What I love about Solomon is the way he got his wisdom. In my opinion, his asking for it displayed an existing wisdom which far exceeds anything I could ever hope to attain! Of course, as is so often true with our biblical heroes, things did turn a bit pear-shaped later on and it is well worth doing an overview reading of Solomon's life to familiarise yourself with his character.

I have scripted this using a courtroom setting, giving it a modern context without altering the Scripture reading. I have given an optional introduction to illustrate this more clearly.

Cast: NARRATOR, SOLOMON, ONE, TWO.

Props: Desk. Three chairs. Gavel. Sword.

THE READING

(*Desk and chair centre stage,* ONE *and* TWO *are seated on either side.* NARRATOR *enters.*)

NARR: (*Optional introduction*) Court in session. All rise . . . the honourable King Solomon presiding.

(SOLOMON *enters and sits centrally behind desk while* ONE *and* TWO *stand respectfully. All sit down once he has settled.*)

NARR: Now two prostitutes came to the king and stood before him. One of them said,

ONE: (*Stands to plead*) My lord, this woman and I live in the same house. I had a baby while she was there with me. The third day after my child was born, this woman also had a baby. We were alone; there was no-one in the house but the two of us.

During the night this woman's son died because she lay on him. So she got up in the middle of the night and took my son from my side while I your servant was asleep. She put him by her breast and put her dead son by my breast.

The next morning, I got up to nurse my son – and he was dead! But when I looked at him closely in the morning light, I saw that it wasn't the son I had borne.

NARR: The other woman said,

TWO: (*Affronted*) No! The living one is my son; the dead one is yours.

NARR: But the first one insisted,

ONE: No! The dead one is yours; the living one is mine.

NARR: And so they argued before the king.

SOLOMON: (*Banging gavel for order*) This one says, 'My son is alive and your son is dead,' while that one says, 'No! Your son is dead and mine is alive.' Bring me a sword.

NARR: (*Fetches sword as he speaks*) So they brought a sword for the king. He then gave an order,

SOLOMON: (*Brandishing weapon*) Cut the living child in two and give half to one and half to the other.

NARR: (*Aside to audience*) The woman whose son was
           alive was filled with compassion for her son and
           said to the king,

ONE: (*Tearfully*) Please, my lord, give her the living
           baby! Don't kill him!

NARR: (*Knowingly*) But the other said,

TWO: (*Smugly*) Neither I nor you shall have him. Cut
           him in two!

SOLOMON: (*Pause, smiling*) Give the living baby to the first
           woman. Do not kill him; she is his mother.

(TWO *storms out;* ONE *thanks* SOLOMON.)

NARR: When all Israel heard the verdict the king had
           given, they held the king in awe, because they
           saw that he had wisdom from God to adminis-
           ter justice.

NOTES

A quick note on the stage instruction called 'aside to audience'. This is a great tool, which can be used to keep an
audience informed of what is going on and how any particular character feels about a situation, even if it is not vocal-
ised. The reader should literally turn to the audience and
speak as if confiding in them – the other characters are obliv-
ious to what is being said, and time during the 'aside' effectively stands still. It can also be used in many instances to
great comic effect.

14. Job's First Test

IN A NUTSHELL

Job is one of those mammoth books, with so much dramatic content it's hard to know where to start when making a selection for a single dramatised reading. I've always thought it would take an epic three-hour movie with Anthony Hopkins in the lead truly to do it justice! Anyway, due to the lack of Sir Anthony and a sixty-million-pound budget, I decided the best place to start was the beginning, so chapter 1 and the very first test it is. This passage also provides an interesting interplay between God and Satan.

Job is God's most obedient servant, and he is put to the ultimate test after God allows Satan to bring great suffering upon him. (Note Satan's accountability to God.) Job is not afraid to show his grief at his immense loss, and the high emotion displays his very human side. It opens a period of soul-searching, on which Job embarks with the aid of some rather questionable friends.

I've scripted this for four readers, though it works very well for a single reader using the technique of basic character voices. Satan also plays the part of the messengers as he is, in effect, the reason for all the calamitous reports.

Cast: NARRATOR, GOD, SATAN, JOB.

Props: Three chairs. Book.

THE READING

(JOB *sits centre stage happily reading.* GOD *sits behind him in an elevated position, with* SATAN *to his side.*)

NARR: One day the angels came to present themselves before the Lord, and Satan also came with them. The Lord said to Satan,

GOD: Where have you come from?

SATAN: From roaming the earth and going to and fro in it.

GOD: Have you considered my servant Job? (*Indicates him proudly*) There is no-one on earth like him; he is blameless and upright, a man who fears God and shuns evil.

SATAN: (*Mocking*) Does Job fear God for nothing? Have you not put a hedge around him and his household and everything he has?

You have blessed the work of his hands, so that his flocks and herds are spread throughout the land. (*Challenging*) But stretch out your hand and strike everything he has, and he will surely curse you to your face.

GOD: (*Pause*) Very well, then, everything he has is in your hands, but on the man himself do not lay a finger.

NARR: Then Satan went out from the presence of the Lord.

(SATAN *exits with a smug smile.*)

One day when Job's sons and daughters were feasting and drinking wine at the oldest brother's house, a messenger came to Job and said,

SATAN: (*Approaches* JOB, *as messenger*) The oxen were ploughing and the donkeys were grazing nearby, and the Sabeans attacked and carried them off. They put the servants to the sword, and I am the only one who has escaped to tell you!

NARR: While he was still speaking, another messenger came and said,

SATAN: (*Goes to other side of* JOB, *as second messenger*) The fire of God fell from the sky and burned up the sheep and the servants, and I am the only one who has escaped to tell you!

NARR: While he was still speaking, another messenger came and said,

SATAN: (*As third messenger*) The Chaldeans formed three raiding parties and swept down on your camels and carried them off. They put the servants to the sword, and I am the only one who has escaped to tell you!

NARR: While he was still speaking, yet another messenger came and said,

SATAN: (*As fourth and most grave messenger*) Your sons and daughters were feasting and drinking wine at the oldest brother's house, when suddenly a mighty wind swept in from the desert and struck the four corners of the house. It collapsed on them and they are dead, and I am the only one who has escaped to tell you!

(*Pause,* SATAN *slowly exits, grinning.*)

NARR: At this, Job got up and tore his robe and shaved his head. Then he fell to the ground in worship and said:

JOB: (*On knees*) Naked I came from my mother's womb, and naked I shall depart. The Lord gave and the Lord has taken away; may the name of the Lord be praised.

NARR: In all this, Job did not sin by charging God with wrongdoing.

PSALM 23

15. A Psalm of David

IN A NUTSHELL

This is another timeless classic which, to be honest, would have been rather conspicuous in its absence. This one is so famous that it virtually trips off the tongue – a great testament to its beauty, but presenting obvious disadvantages. The advantage is that we know and love the psalm, and the congregation will very likely be familiar with it too. The disadvantage is that we are so familiar with it that we read it in a dreamy singsong rhythm and miss out a lot of the meaning.

In this scripting for a solo reader, I have attempted to communicate where David was both physically and emotionally. This is done with the minimum of action, but with changes in vocal style. I guarantee that the more times you read this out loud prior to performance, the more real it will become.

Cast: DAVID.

Props: Sound FX: nature/birdsong.

THE READING

(DAVID *sits centre stage, eyes closed. Sound FX: nature/birdsong. He opens his eyes to speak, he is very calm. The first few verses are spoken slowly and meaningfully, leaving a brief pause between each statement.*)

DAVID: The Lord is my shepherd, I shall not be in want.
                He makes me lie down in green pastures,

he leads me beside quiet waters,
he restores my soul.
He guides me in paths of righteousness
for his name's sake.

(*Adopt a slightly graver tone.*)

Even though I walk
through the valley of the shadow of death,
I will fear no evil,

(*Become more upbeat and positive as a result of God's promise.*)

for you are with me;
your rod and your staff,
they comfort me.

(*Slightly change direction or position. Switch to a more up-tempo vocal style, imagining you are telling a story.*)

You prepare a table for me
in the presence of my enemies.
You anoint my head with oil;
my cup overflows.

(*The final verses express hope – not a blind hope, but an assured hope of what is to come.*)

Surely goodness and love will follow me
all the days of my life,
and I will dwell in the house of the Lord
for ever.

(*Sound FX: birdsong. Play for a few seconds and then fade to end.*)

NOTES

A congregation is not expecting to hear anything new in a reading of Psalm 23, but if you can translate something of David's emotions, your listeners will begin to experience the way God can use the reading of Scripture to communicate powerfully.

PSALM 139

16. Another Psalm of David

IN A NUTSHELL

This is another favourite psalm and, like Psalm 23, I think it comes over best read by a single reader. When we look into the emotions behind it there is so much to uncover, and concentrating on that is how I believe we can best communicate it.

David, as we know, was a man of real spiritual highs and lows. In this psalm he challenges us to do as he does, which is to ask God to search out our hidden sin and point it out to us, even to test our private thoughts. When we do this and God reveals areas of sin to us, it can be a hard process, but when we repent we can expect God's full forgiveness. That is the challenge when reading this piece – to cause the listener to say to God, 'Search me and know my heart.'

Cast: DAVID.

Props: Sound FX: background music. Chair.

THE READING

(DAVID *is seated centre stage in deep thought. Quiet music is heard in the background.*)

DAVID:　　　(*Continuing in deep thought, speak quietly*) O Lord, you have searched me (*Pause*) and you know me. You know when I sit and when I rise;

(At this point stand; the music that has been playing reaches a crescendo, then stops suddenly.)

you perceive my thoughts from afar. You discern my going out and my lying down; you are familiar with all my ways. Before a word is on my tongue *(Click fingers)* you know it completely, O Lord.

(Step up the tempo from meditative mode to awestruck.)

You hem me in – behind and before; you have laid your hand upon me. *(Absolute awe)* Such knowledge is too wonderful for me, too lofty for me to attain.

(Imploring to heavens) Where can I go from your Spirit? Where can I flee from your presence? *(Rising inflection to ask questions)* If I go up to the heavens, *(Pause, change in tone for answers)* you are there; if I make my bed in the depths, you are there.

If I rise on the wings of the dawn, if I settle on the far side of the sea, even there your hand will guide me, your right hand will hold me fast. If I say, *(Change tone to speak quote)* 'Surely the darkness will hide me and the light become night around me,' *(Revert to normal voice, amazed at God's power)* even the darkness will not be dark to you; the night will shine like the day, for darkness is as light to you.

(Sit back down, remaining in total amazement at God's power. Pause for thought.)

(*Quietly*) For you created my inmost being; you knit me together in my mother's womb. I praise you because I am fearfully and wonderfully made; your works are wonderful, I know that full well.

My frame was not hidden from you when I was made in the secret place. When I was woven together in the depths of the earth, your eyes saw my unformed body. All the days ordained for me were written in your book before one of them came to be.

(*Slowly raise the tempo*) How precious to me are your thoughts, O God! How vast is the sum of them! Were I to count them, they would out-number the grains of sand. When I awake, I am still with you.

(*His thoughts turn to the wicked and those who hate God.*)

(*Rise in righteous anger*) If only you would slay the wicked, O God! Away from me, you blood-thirsty men! They speak of you with evil intent; your adversaries misuse your name. (*With venom*) Do I not hate those who hate you, O Lord, and abhor those who rise up against you? I have nothing but hatred for them; I count them my enemies.

(*Sit back down. Having vented his fury,* DAVID *acknowledges that justice and vengeance is God's alone. Yes, he can cry to God to intervene, but in these situations he should concentrate on letting God deal with his shortcomings. Quiet music begins again.*)

(*Quietly*) Search me, O God, and know my heart; test me and know my anxious thoughts.

See if there is any offensive way in me, and lead
me in the way everlasting.

(DAVID *has a satisfied smile, music slowly fades.*)

17. Everything Is Meaningless

IN A NUTSHELL

Have you ever felt a bit restless or frustrated, wondering what the point of it all is and if you're in God's will or just bumbling along? Well, join Solomon's club! As you read this passage you sense his utter boredom and dissatisfaction as he mulls over his achievements in life.

The writings are in effect a warning. Solomon realises that all the things he's done in life, the meaningless pursuits and other accomplishments, have given him no earthly pleasure. His only pleasure, as he concludes later in the book, is in God. By the way, it is well worth doing an overview reading of the book so you see more than just the pessimism. The only thing that will ultimately give satisfaction and mean anything in the realms of time is pursuing the will of God.

Scripted for one reader, the challenge here is to communicate utter boredom and dissatisfaction. Although laced with pathos, this can also be quite funny. Of course that is not the overall teaching of the book, but, coupled with teaching on what gives us our craving for satisfaction, it can come over very powerfully. Purely as a dramatic reading for one reader, it is one of my favourite passages in the Bible.

Cast: SOLOMON.

Props: Sound FX: ticking clock. Chair. Books (optional). Pack of cards or other game for Solomon to fiddle with idly.

THE READING

(SOLOMON *is seated looking utterly bored. He is surrounded by things of pleasure (books, perhaps) but they do not curb his boredom. Maybe a clock is ticking behind him. Perhaps* SOLOMON *could be flicking cards into an upturned hat a few feet in front of him. Whatever you decide, before he speaks the listener is in no doubt that he is very bored!*)

SOLOMON: (*Suddenly and loudly*) 'Meaningless! Meaningless!' says the Teacher. (*Indicates himself*) 'Utterly meaningless! Everything is meaningless.'

(*Pause, then questions audience*) What does man gain from all his labour at which he toils under the sun? (*Awaits answer, none is forthcoming*) Generations come and generations go, but the earth remains for ever.

(*Exaggerated mime of the sun*) The sun rises and the sun sets, and hurries back to where it rises. The wind blows to the south and turns to the north; round and round it goes, ever returning on its course. All streams flow into the sea, (*Sarcastic*) yet the sea is never full. To the place the streams come from, there they return again.

(*Pause, then shouts out*) All things are wearisome, more than one can say. The eye never has enough of seeing, nor the ear its fill of hearing. (*Stretching out words like a bored teenager, with utter contempt*) What has been will be again, what has been done will be done again; there is nothing new under the sun.

(*Change of thought*) Is there anything of which one can say, (*Use different voice, with note of sarcasm*) 'Look! This is something new'?

(*Dismissing*) It was here already, long ago; it was here before our time. (*Poignantly*) There is no remembrance of men of old, and even those who are yet to come will not be remembered by those who follow.

(*Storytelling mode*) I, the Teacher, was king over Israel in Jerusalem. I devoted myself to study (*Indicate books*) and to explore by wisdom all that is done under heaven. What a heavy burden God has laid on men! I have seen all the things that are done under the sun; all of them are (*Shouts*) meaningless, a chasing after the wind.

(*Clears throat to deliver profound thought*) What is twisted cannot be straightened; What is lacking cannot be counted.

(*Knowing pause, smiling at his brilliance, which fades into a dismissive, 'forget it' wave of the hand. Then, thoughtfully*) I thought to myself, 'Look, I have grown and increased in wisdom more than anyone who has ruled over Jerusalem before me; I have experienced much of wisdom and knowledge.'

Then I applied myself to the understanding of wisdom, (*Aside*) and also of madness and folly, but I learned that this, too, is a chasing after the wind. (*Pause*) For with much wisdom comes much sorrow; the more knowledge, the more grief.

(*Deep sigh, then he continues his actions at beginning of reading with expression of boredom.*)

ECCLESIASTES 3:1–8

18. A Time for Everything

IN A NUTSHELL

I've put this one in as a do-it-yourself reading! When it comes to dramatising Scripture with wild actions or with groups of children, we don't have to look much further than this passage. It gives us plenty of opportunity for interesting and often funny mimes. If I'm totally honest, dramatising Scripture in this way is not my particular preference, but I admit it can be fun, so here goes.

In our enthusiasm to get miming, let's not forget the challenge to apply some understanding of the Scripture. The key ingredient is to communicate timing (hence the ticking clock in the stage directions). Things are relevant at certain times and in certain situations; the challenge is to discern these and find God's perfect timing.

I've purposely left the directions incredibly loose on this one – so get a team together, get creative, and get miming!

Cast: NARRATOR, ENSEMBLE (up to about eight).

Props: Sound FX: ticking clock; alarm; ambulance siren (optional). Stones (optional). Bag of sweets. Paper and sticky tape.

THE READING

(ENSEMBLE *stand in a row across stage, heads bowed. Sound FX: loud ticking clock followed by alarm. At the alarm the* ENSEMBLE *look up with a sudden start.*)

NARR: There is a time for everything, and a season for
             every activity under heaven: a time to be born
             and a time to die,

*(Actions after each phrase: punchy, and don't be afraid to use
loud screams!)*

             a time to plant and a time to uproot,

(Action: possibly one half of ENSEMBLE *planting, the other half
annoyingly uprooting.)*

             a time to kill and a time to heal,

*(Action: use lots of facial expressions for killing, possible use
of ambulance siren for healing.)*

             a time to tear down and a time to build,

*(Action: come up with something funny and original – prefer-
ably not someone falling down then getting back up again.)*

             a time to weep and a time to laugh,

*(Keep the actions loud, punchy and very definite. The laugh
comes from the quick change from one extreme to the
other.)*

             a time to mourn and a time to dance,

*(Action: use anything from a brief hop and skip to a well-
choreographed masterpiece that could be the envy of Britney!)*

             a time to scatter stones and a time to gather
             them,

(*Action: maybe have half the group throwing stones around, while the other half pick them up getting increasingly frustrated.*)

a time to embrace and a time to refrain,

(*Action: hug then part.*)

a time to search and a time to give up,

(*Action: punchy and over-the-top searching and giving up.*)

a time to keep and a time to throw away,

(*Action: have a bag of sweets that you hog, then generously throw into congregation – this goes down very well!*)

a time to tear and a time to mend,

(*Action: sheets of paper and sticky tape – need I say more?*)

a time to be silent

(*Uncomfortable pause, all looking blankly at each other.*)

and a time to speak,

(*Start chatting in relief, 'Ooh, about time too!'*)

a time to love and a time to hate,

(*Action: this can be done in any one of a thousand ways, from the serious to the ridiculous. Experiment creatively with a few of the group's ideas.*)

a time for war and a time for peace.

(*Action: again, lots of options here. As it is the last couplet, be sure to end with a strong final pose. Hold the pose for a few seconds, then all* ENSEMBLE *exit, half to left and half to right.*)

NOTES

The directions I have given here are merely suggestions, and you can do literally hundreds of actions to match the text. Use this exercise in a drama workshop, by splitting the group into smaller teams and challenging them to come up with some ideas before showing them to the rest of the group. Give the groups the Bible passage only, and no suggested directions at all. It's interesting to see the different things people come up with, and also what they do that is exactly the same.

A small tip when doing actions during a narrated piece: keep the movements short, snappy and punchy. Use lots of facial expression and a variety of vocal sound effects. At the end of each action hold onto a freeze, which you only break when moving into the next movement. This gives the piece much more pace and a slicker overall feel.

ISAIAH 40:21–31

19. Isaiah Comforts God's People

IN A NUTSHELL

In my poll to collate favourite readings for inclusion in this book, this passage weighed in with quite a few votes, and no wonder. It's a real powerhouse of a reading. From a dramatic perspective it's also brilliantly written and structured. Whatever people may believe, you cannot dispute that the Bible is the most brilliantly written book and a pleasure to read.

Amazing as it seems, God does not tire of our requests – he never puts us on hold or says, 'Come back tomorrow.' God will renew our strength, as this passage explains, and we should therefore deliver these words with appropriate excitement and awe.

Scripted with lots of vocal ideas for a solo reader, this piece has the potential to communicate powerfully.

Cast: ISAIAH.

Props: None required.

THE READING

(ISAIAH *sits. Suddenly looks up. Glancing around audience, he stands to address them.*)

ISAIAH: (*Questioning*) Do you not know?

(*Continues to look around, asking questions with increasing passion to different directions.*)

111

Have you not heard? Has it not been told you from the beginning? Have you not understood since the earth was founded?

(*Changes tone to answer questions excitedly.*)

He sits enthroned above the circle of the earth, and its people are like grasshoppers. He stretches out the heavens like a canopy, and spreads them out like a tent to live in. He brings princes to naught and reduces the rulers of this world to nothing.

(*Up the tempo for verse 24, concentrating on how God's power is so much greater than anything else; how, compared to him, things pale into insignificance.*)

No sooner are they planted, no sooner are they sown, no sooner do they take root in the ground, than he blows on them and they wither, and a whirlwind sweeps them away like chaff.

(*Pause. Hold back on these lines, reading them in softer tones.*)

'To whom will you compare me? Or who is my equal?' says the Holy One. Lift your eyes and look to the heavens: Who created all these?

(*Short pause. Change of tone to answer previous questions.*)

He who brings out the starry host one by one, and calls them each by name. Because of his great power and mighty strength, not one of them is missing.

(Change of tone as he mocks the complaining of the Israelites. Use the voice of a real whiner in verse 27b.)

> Why do you say, O Jacob, and complain, O Israel, *(Whining)* 'My way is hidden from the Lord; my cause is disregarded by my God'?

(Note the beginning of verse 28 is the same as verse 21, so deliver it in the same way, as if coming full circle.)

> Do you not know? Have you not heard?

(Closing few verses should be delivered with excitement again. Once you understand the truth of what you are saying, about God strengthening the weak, the hope we have in the Lord, and soaring on wings like eagles, summoning the required degree of excitement shouldn't be too tricky!)

> The Lord is the everlasting God, the Creator of the ends of the earth. He will not grow tired or weary, and his understanding no-one can fathom. He gives strength to the weary and increases the power of the weak.
> Even youths grow tired and weary, and young men stumble and fall; but those who hope in the Lord will renew their strength. They will soar on wings like eagles; they will run and not grow weary, they will walk and not be faint.

NOTES

In this reading I have offered direction to change tone numerous times, so here's a quick note on this. When we talk we constantly have 'changes of thought' – sometimes we say something and it reminds us of something else, or someone else adds to a discussion, sending us off on a different train of thought. This is demonstrated vocally by a change in tone, whether we realise it or not. Failing to do this when we read out loud means that we fall into the trap of becoming monotone.

It is very hard to explain this in writing, but for a simple example, imagine a basic two-way conversation.

Question: 'What time are we going to the cinema?'

Answer: 'Just after eight o'clock.'

If you act out these lines a few times, you will notice you use different tones. Now try to say the answer using the same tone you use for the question, and vice versa. You should hear that it doesn't sound right. With practice and by actively listening to everyday conversations, this skill of vocal variation should become more natural.

20. Jonah Flees from the Lord

IN A NUTSHELL

The story of Jonah, his fleeing from God and eventual mission to Nineveh (via a torrid sea cruise with seventy-two hour stopover in a whale's gut) is one of the most famous and enduring in the Old Testament. It has great visual imagery and is laced with humour and evidence of that all-too-recognisable human frailty. There is without doubt much to learn from Jonah's tale.

In this chapter we see our intrepid prophet flagrantly disobeying God's command to go to Nineveh, the wicked capital city of the Assyrian Empire. It wasn't just fear that stopped him going, but also an intense hatred of the Assyrians, whom he didn't feel warranted God's mercy. Through a series of costly lessons, Jonah learns that running away from God is futile and that no-one is beyond redemption.

Cast: ONE, TWO.

Props: Sound FX: opening music; storm sounds. Two signs, one reading 'Nineveh' with an arrow pointing right, the other 'Tarshish' with an arrow pointing left. Straws of varying lengths.

THE READING

(*Opening music.* ONE *and* TWO *enter.* ONE *stands on one side of stage,* TWO *sits on the other side, sleeping. The music stops abruptly and* TWO *is woken suddenly from his sleep.*)

ONE: The word of the Lord came to Jonah son of
              Amittai: (*Slight pause, then turn to* TWO) 'Go to
              the great city of Nineveh and preach against it,
              because its wickedness has come up before
              me.'

(TWO *holds up two signs, one with 'Nineveh' and arrow point-*
ing to right, the second with 'Tarshish' and arrow pointing to
left. TWO *pauses for thought and then throws the Nineveh sign*
over his shoulder.)

TWO: But Jonah ran away from the Lord and headed
              for Tarshish. He went down to Joppa, where he
              found a ship bound for that port. After paying
              the fare, he went aboard and sailed for
              Tarshish to flee from the Lord. (TWO *resumes*
              sleep)

(*Sound FX: storm.*)

ONE: Then the Lord sent a great wind on the sea, and
              such a violent storm arose that the ship threat-
              ened to break up. All the sailors were afraid and
              each cried out to his own god. And they threw
              the cargo into the sea to lighten the ship. But
              Jonah had gone below deck, where he lay down
              and fell into a deep sleep.

              (ONE *looks witheringly towards the sleeping*
              TWO) The captain went to him and said, 'How
              can you sleep? Get up and call on your god!
              Maybe he will take notice of us, and we will not
              perish.' Then the sailors said to each other,
              'Come, let us cast lots to find out who is respon-
              sible for this calamity.' They cast lots . . .

(TWO *holds up a handful of straws, takes a deep breath, then draws a very short one. He looks suitably worried.*)

... and the lot fell on Jonah.

TWO: (*Delivered in a tone that indicates he is rather fed up and nagged*) So they asked him, 'Tell us, who is responsible for making all this trouble for us? What do you do? Where do you come from? What is your country? From what people are you?' He answered, (*Slight pause, then deliver with authority*) 'I am a Hebrew and I worship the Lord, the God of heaven, who made the sea and the land.'

ONE: (*To audience*) This terrified them and they asked, (*To* TWO) 'What have you done?' (*Aside to audience*) They knew he was running away from the Lord, because he had already told them so.

TWO: The sea was getting rougher and rougher. So they asked him, (*Mimic panicked voices*) 'What should we do to you to make the sea calm down for us?' (*Slight pause*) 'Pick me up and throw me into the sea,' he replied, 'and it will become calm. I know that it is my fault that this great storm has come upon you.'

(*Bring up high sound FX of storm.*)

ONE: (*Frantic*) Instead, the men did their best to row back to land. But they could not, for the sea grew even wilder than before. Then they cried to the Lord, 'O Lord, please do not let us die for taking this man's life. Do not hold us accountable for killing an innocent man, for you, O Lord, have done as you pleased.'

TWO: (*Voice raised above loud storm*) Then they took Jonah and threw him overboard, (TWO *throws head into arms and the storm suddenly stops. Silent pause*)

ONE: and the raging sea grew calm. At this the men greatly feared the Lord, and they offered a sacrifice to the Lord and made vows to him.

TWO: (*Slowly raises head with a look of disgust*) But the Lord provided a great fish to swallow Jonah, and Jonah was inside the fish three days and three nights.

(*Reprise a short section of the opening music as* ONE *and* TWO *exit.*)

PART 2

New Testament

21. The Birth of Jesus

IN A NUTSHELL

Dramatically, the story of Christ's birth is one of the most enduring in Scripture. Countless plays and sketches have been based on it, viewing the story from less familiar angles, or getting under the skin of different characters.

When performing the text as a reading, we are obviously limiting ourselves strictly to the actual words of Scripture, but this can offer a traditional telling coupled with a strong vocal reading. Rather than mount an elaborate dramatisation, I have scripted this as a narrated reading with certain lines additionally taken by an acting ensemble. The reading is split into three sections, each staged like a picture postcard, using a 'freeze-frame' image and minimal movement. If you have access to lighting, it would be very effective to use different settings to indicate each particular scene.

Cast: NARRATOR (plus acting ensemble to include MARY, JOSEPH, ANGEL, HEROD, PRIEST, MAGI).

Props: Sound FX: music for between scenes. Lights. Scroll. Manger and nativity scene. Star. Magi's gifts (optional).

THE READING

(*Open with appropriate music. Lights up on a pregnant* MARY *seated with* JOSEPH *behind, his hand on her shoulder.* ANGEL *stands a few feet behind* JOSEPH, *not in traditional costume –*

121

maybe a man in a suit. NARRATOR *is positioned at the side of the stage.*)

NARR: This is how the birth of Jesus Christ came about: His mother Mary was pledged to be married to Joseph, but before they came together, she was found to be with child through the Holy Spirit.

Because Joseph her husband was a righteous man and did not want to expose her to public disgrace, he had in mind to divorce her quietly.

But after he had considered this, an angel of the Lord appeared to him in a dream and said,

ANGEL: (*Steps forward and speaks to* JOSEPH, *whose eyes are closed. Tone is calming and friendly*) Joseph son of David, do not be afraid to take Mary home as your wife, because what is conceived in her is from the Holy Spirit. She will give birth to a son, and you are to give him the name Jesus, because he will save his people from their sins.

NARR: All this took place to fulfil what the Lord had said through the prophet: 'The virgin will be with child and will give birth to a son, and they will call him Immanuel' – which means, 'God with us.'

(ANGEL *resumes opening position,* JOSEPH *opens eyes.*)

When Joseph woke up, he did what the angel of the Lord had commanded him and took Mary home as his wife. But he had no union with her until she gave birth to a son. And he gave him the name Jesus.

(JOSEPH *and* MARY *exit, followed by* ANGEL. *Short pause with music. In blackout, enter* HEROD, PRIEST *and two* MAGI. *They stand in freeze-frame,* MAGI *slightly further upstage.*)

	After Jesus was born in Bethlehem in Judea, during the time of King Herod, Magi from the east came to Jerusalem and asked,
MAGI:	Where is the one who has been born king of the Jews? We saw his star in the east and have come to worship him.
HEROD:	When King Herod heard this he was disturbed, and all Jerusalem with him. When he had called together all the people's chief priests and teachers of the law, he asked them where the Christ was to be born.
PRIEST:	In Bethlehem in Judea, for this is what the prophet has written: (*Reading from a scroll*) 'But you, Bethlehem, in the land of Judah, are by no means least among the rulers of Judah; for out of you will come a ruler who will be the shepherd of my people Israel.'
NARR:	Then Herod called the Magi secretly and found out from them the exact time the star had appeared. He sent them to Bethlehem and said,
HEROD:	(*Smarmy*) Go and make a careful search for the child. As soon as you find him, report to me, so that I too may go and worship him.

(*Short pause, then music. In blackout* HEROD *and* PRIEST *exit,* MARY *and* JOSEPH *enter with traditional manger and nativity scene.* MAGI *stay in position onstage.*)

NARR:	After they had heard the king, they went on their way, and the star they had seen in the east (*If possible illuminate a star either with a prop or*

visual aid) went ahead of them until it stopped over the place where the child was.

When they saw the star, they were overjoyed. On coming to the house, they saw the child with his mother Mary, and they bowed down and worshipped him. (MAGI *bow and kneel*)

Then they opened their treasures and presented him with gifts of gold and of incense and of myrrh. (*Picture postcard freeze-frame*)

And having been warned in a dream not to go back to Herod, they returned to their country by another route.

(*Blackout and closing music. All exit.*)

NOTES

In this piece I have scripted a lot of freeze-frames. You may think that seems a little boring, but if done well stillness onstage is highly effective. I have given no strict direction on exactly how to create your freeze-frame, but have allowed you to be creative and come up with some original positions. Remember, it is not just the positions that will communicate, but the expressions too.

As a warm-up with your group, try out this easy freeze-frame exercise. Break into groups and choose an emotion. Think of a suitable situation, and communicate that emotion in a single freeze-frame position. Don't be afraid to be 'arty' – imagine your freeze-frame as a clay model. Simply moving a person a foot to the left or right, or to a slightly different angle, can for some reason be all the more pleasing to the eye. Some emotions you can use for this exercise are fear, love, anger, excitement and sadness. Having done a few practices, you will be raring to go, thinking about positions and emotions to communicate the different views of Christ's birth.

MATTHEW 4:1-11

22. The Temptation of Jesus

IN A NUTSHELL

The temptation of Jesus reads like the ultimate game of chess, a battle of wits between two great minds. Satan enters at a moment when Christ is experiencing apparent physical weakness, and tries to outfox his enemy. Obviously there was only ever one winner, but to give the story its full meaning we must sense a real tension between the two, not a feeling that it is all a foregone conclusion. Satan, after all, must have thought he had a chance of victory!

In the story Jesus refuses to put God to the test, even when Satan starts quoting from Scripture, attempting to make it support his twisted view – unfortunately a practice still visible in the church today.

This reading really needs to be performed. In a straight reading it is easy to lose the tension, but by turning it into a simple dramatisation we have the opportunity to communicate what lies between the lines.

Cast: NARRATOR, JESUS, SATAN.

Props: Bowl of water (optional). Stone.

THE READING

(JESUS *is sitting on floor centre stage. He looks weak and is slurping water from his hands.*)

NARR: Then Jesus was led by the Spirit into the desert to be tempted by the devil. After fasting for forty days and forty nights, he was hungry. The tempter came to him and said,

SATAN: (*Enters slowly and stands by* JESUS) If you are the Son of God, tell these stones to become bread.

(SATAN *drops a stone at* JESUS' *feet.* JESUS *picks it up to examine it, then stands to face* SATAN.)

JESUS: It is written: 'Man does not live on bread alone, but on every word that comes from the mouth of God.' (*He throws stone to the ground*)

NARR: Then the devil took him to the holy city and had him stand on the highest point of the temple.

(SATAN *leads* JESUS *stage right.*)

SATAN: If you are the Son of God, throw yourself down. For it is written: (*Spoken with a sarcastic, dramatic flourish*) 'He will command his angels concerning you, and they will lift you up in their hands, so that you will not strike your foot against a stone.'

JESUS: It is also written: 'Do not put the Lord your God to the test.'

NARR: Again, the devil took him to a very high mountain and showed him all the kingdoms of the world and their splendour.

SATAN: (*Sincerely*) All this I will give you, if you will bow down and worship me.

JESUS: Away from me, Satan! For it is written: 'Worship the Lord your God, and serve him only.'

(*Few seconds' pause as* SATAN *stares at* JESUS. *He then smiles, realising he will not turn* JESUS, *and exits.*)

NARR: Then the devil left him, and angels came and attended him.

NOTES

Learning Scripture off by heart to read in church is, in reality, probably too time-consuming. In a piece like this, however, the readers taking the parts of Jesus and Satan might consider learning the words so that they can concentrate on acting it out rather than constantly looking down to the text. The number of words spoken by each is minimal when you take away the narrated portions, which don't need to be learnt, and it could potentially add much impact to the reading.

23. The Beatitudes

IN A NUTSHELL

As in Ecclesiastes 3, the Beatitudes in Matthew 5 lend themselves to a narrated mime performance. Although not the most powerful way to communicate a reading, it does have the advantage of getting a group to think carefully about the text and then use their creative skills to communicate it.

At this point Jesus is not preaching to the crowds. Read the verses before to see how, after healing the sick and attracting a vast crowd, he goes up the mountainside with his disciples to sit down for some peace and quiet. The text indicates that he is speaking to them here, not the crowd.

Any mimed narrative such as this will inevitably cause ripples of laughter; it can prove incredibly difficult to keep this style free of humour. I would suggest that, from verse 10 on, you aim to make a strong final impression rather than leaving 'em laughing! The piece should begin as it ends, with the disciples sitting around Jesus listening to him, crowd noise audible in the background.

Cast: JESUS (as narrator), DISCIPLES (ensemble of around 4–8).

Props: Sound FX: crowd noises.

THE READING

(*Sound FX: crowd noises.* JESUS *and* DISCIPLES *enter looking extremely tired and all flake out on the mountainside. Fade out crowd noises.*)

JESUS: (*Narrating*) Now when he saw the crowds, he went up on a mountainside and sat down. His disciples came to him, and he began to teach them, saying:

(*On the word 'saying', the ensemble stands to assume first positions. Remember not to have everyone standing in a straight line, but give the positions an interesting depth and shape. See note on narrated pieces following the reading from Ecclesiastes 3, page 110.*)

Blessed are the poor in spirit, for theirs is the kingdom of heaven.

(*Short action to represent poor. Freeze.*)

Blessed are those who mourn, for they will be comforted.

(*Short action for mourning and comforting – you can either have all the ensemble doing both quickly, or have half mourning and half comforting. Freeze.*)

Blessed are the meek, for they will inherit the earth.

(*Short action to represent meek. Discuss beforehand with your group the qualities in a meek person and settle on a suitable action. Freeze.*)

Blessed are those who hunger and thirst for righteousness, for they will be filled.

(*Short action for both hunger and thirst or righteousness. If you choose hunger, the point can still be made this way,*

*although it's not strictly speaking about physical hunger.
Freeze.)*

> Blessed are the merciful, for they will be shown
> mercy.

(Short action for mercy. Freeze.)

> Blessed are the pure in heart, for they will see
> God.

(Short action for purity – angelic poses, or similar. Freeze.)

> Blessed are the peacemakers, for they will be
> called sons of God.

*(Short action for peace. Wide variety of options depending on
style used and potential audience. The two-finger hippy thing
is very popular, but possibly a bit overused! Freeze.)*

> Blessed are those who are persecuted because
> of righteousness, for theirs is the kingdom of
> heaven.

(Strong freeze-frame depicting persecution.)

> Blessed are you when people insult you, perse-
> cute you and falsely say all kinds of evil against
> you because of me.

*(During this verse, ensemble holds previous persecution freeze-
frame, then individuals move one or two at a time within this
position. For instance, as Jesus says 'when people insult you',
one or two can break the freeze to change position and spit at
the persecuted. In effect, you create a moving picture.)*

Rejoice and be glad,

(JESUS *moves to a central standing position. As he finishes the verse, one at a time the ensemble return to sitting position, listening to* JESUS. *You will need to decide exactly who sits when, and where they will go.*)

because great is your reward in heaven, for in the same way they persecuted the prophets who were before you.

(JESUS *looks at his disciples. Slowly bring back up the crowd noise sound FX.*)

24. Jesus Walks on the Water

IN A NUTSHELL

Jesus' feat of walking on the water is possibly the most famous of his many miracles. It is well worth reading the preceding chapter to understand a little of Jesus' state of mind at this point. He has just heard of the beheading of his beloved John the Baptist, and he wants to find a place of solitude. Instead, Jesus is immediately thrust into the crowds, famously feeding the five thousand and displaying his overwhelming compassion for the sick. At this point our reading begins, and once more Jesus is seeking – successfully this time – a quiet spot to pray.

This in itself is a challenge for us. If Jesus found it necessary to spend time alone with God the Father, how important must it be for us too. In the passage we must not paint Peter as testing Jesus, but rather as falteringly exercising his faith. As with our own attempts at increasing our faith, when Peter concentrated on the problem, he sank, but when he focused on the solution, he was rescued.

I have scripted this piece for a single reader, to avoid the problem of trying to act out the walking on water. I have suggested the use of water sound FX to help focus the listeners' attention and to conjure up more vividly the exchange between Jesus and Peter across the water.

Cast: NARRATOR.

Props: Sound FX: different sounds of water and wind, from calm to raging. Blue floodlight (optional).

THE READING

(Sound FX: calm water. If you have the use of lighting, do this reading under a blue floodlight.)

NARR: Immediately Jesus made the disciples get into the boat and go on ahead of him to the other side, while he dismissed the crowd.

After he had dismissed them, he went up on a mountainside by himself to pray.

When evening came, he was there alone, but the boat was already a considerable distance from land, buffeted by the waves because the wind was against it.

(Pause. Sound FX: slightly rougher sea and wind.)

During the fourth watch of the night Jesus went out to them, walking on the lake. *(More urgency in voice)* When the disciples saw him walking on the lake, they were terrified. *(Fearfully)* 'It's a ghost,' they said, and cried out in fear.

But Jesus immediately said to them: *(Calmly)* 'Take courage! It is I. Don't be afraid.' *(Indicate vocal change)* 'Lord, if it's you,' Peter replied, 'tell me to come to you on the water.'

(Pause, then speak as if it were the most natural thing in the world) 'Come,' he said.

(Repeat sound FX of stronger waves and wind.)

(Storytelling mode) Then Peter got down out of the boat, walked on the water and came towards Jesus. *(Distracted)* But when he saw the

wind, he was afraid and, beginning to sink, cried out, 'Lord, save me!'

Immediately Jesus reached out his hand and caught him. 'You of little faith,' he said, 'why did you doubt?'

(*Pause*) And when they climbed into the boat, the wind died down. Then those who were in the boat worshipped him, saying, 'Truly you are the Son of God.'

(*Sound FX: calm waters fading out.*)

25. The Transfiguration

IN A NUTSHELL

It is hard to imagine the nature of the event witnessed by the disciples, and very hard to do any kind of justice to it. How do we communicate the blinding light of Jesus' face? A torch just won't do the trick!

The answer is in Peter's misplaced desire to build a shelter for the three. The transfiguration should not drive us to get busy and do things, but should simply encourage us to worship and admire the majestic nature of God.

With this thought in mind, I have scripted this as a narration with no action onstage, but a series of images to help focus the listeners' thoughts. I have given some suggestions for images and effects you can use, but prayerfully consider the reading first and try to come up with some creative ideas of your own. Try to bring the listeners to a point of meditation in keeping with the theme of worship. This would work well in a service during the time of worship.

Cast: NARRATOR.

Props: Sound FX: natural sounds; recording of God's words from verse 5. Bright light. Sheet on which to project images. Cut-out figures of three people (optional). Images of Jesus, empty tomb and cross. Red filter for light.

THE READING

(*Darkness. Sound FX: sounds of nature. This is in keeping with the opening sequence of climbing a mountain.*)

135

NARR: After six days Jesus took with him Peter, James
               and John the brother of James, and led them up
               a high mountain by themselves. There he was
               transfigured before them.

(*Blinding light shatters the darkness. Try to find the strongest
light you can – a spotlight, car headlight, etc. It should cause
the congregation to look away.*)

               His face shone like the sun, and his clothes
               became as white as the light. Just then there
               appeared before them Moses and Elijah,
               talking with Jesus.

(*At this point shine light behind pre-set sheet. Between the
light and the sheet have either three people or three cut-out
images so that Jesus, Moses and Elijah are presented in
shadow form.*)

               Peter said to Jesus, 'Lord, it is good for us to be
               here. If you wish, I will put up three shelters –
               one for you, one for Moses and one for Elijah.'
               While he was still speaking, a bright cloud
               enveloped them, and a voice from the cloud said,

(*Fade out the light on the three shadows. Different voice from
that of the* NARRATOR *is recorded for the voice of God.*)

VOICE: (*Pre-recorded*) This is my Son, whom I love;
               with him I am well pleased. Listen to him!
NARR: When the disciples heard this, they fell face
               down to the ground, terrified. But Jesus came
               and touched them.

(*Image of Jesus is projected onto screen.*)

'Get up,' he said. 'Don't be afraid.' When they looked up, they saw no-one except Jesus.

As they were coming down the mountain, Jesus instructed them, 'Don't tell anyone what you have seen, until the Son of Man has been raised from the dead.'

(*Change image on screen to one of an empty tomb.*)

The disciples asked him, 'Why then do the teachers of the law say that Elijah must come first?' Jesus replied, 'To be sure, Elijah comes and will restore all things.

'But I tell you, Elijah has already come, and they did not recognise him, but have done to him everything they wished.

(*Pause. Empty tomb image is removed and light shines again behind sheet. This time it shows an image of the cross. If possible, cover the light with a red tint.*)

'In the same way the Son of Man is going to suffer at their hands.' Then the disciples understood that he was talking to them about John the Baptist.

(*Pause. Fade out lights to end.*)

NOTES

Using images onstage can be very powerful, and can also be an interesting creative exercise. Linked with the reading, think about types of music you could use, applicable sound effects, images created onstage using light, basic props and projected images. When conducting a creative experiment like this, you will find that trying things out will prove much more fruitful than sitting around talking about it for hours. With trial and error you will be able to create some very powerful sequences.

26. The Parable of the Unmerciful Servant

IN A NUTSHELL

I have written this script as a play within a play. In the first
story Peter comes to ask Jesus for advice, and further characters enact Jesus' answer. Note that this could potentially
cause confusion if it is not done well. Except for Peter and
Jesus, the characters are fictional, active only in the parable
Jesus tells, so you can create them on stage rather like
puppets, with Jesus as the puppeteer. At the beginning they
are frozen in position and only come alive at Jesus' bidding
– he could either point at them or give them a light touch on
the shoulder.

Cast: JESUS, PETER, MASTER, SERVANT 1, SERVANT 2.

Props: Sound FX: opening music. Chair.

THE READING

(*Music plays as cast take opening positions.* JESUS *seated
centre stage. Behind him, standing from left to right, are*
MASTER, *standing upright; slightly further back,* SERVANT 1,
looking worried; and a bit further back, SERVANT 2, *looking
into space.*)

PETER: (*Enters, enquiring*) Then Peter came to Jesus
              and asked, 'Lord, how many times shall I
              forgive my brother when he sins against me? Up
              to seven times?'

JESUS: I tell you, not seven times, but seventy-seven
              times.

(PETER *looks confused,* JESUS *starts to explain.*)

JESUS: Therefore, the kingdom of heaven is like a king
              who wanted to settle accounts with his ser-
              vants.

(*During this verse* JESUS *walks to* MASTER *and touches his
shoulder, breaking his freeze.*)

JESUS: As he began the settlement, a man who owed
              him ten thousand talents was brought to him.

(JESUS *turns* SERVANT 1 *to face* MASTER.)

MASTER: (*Sternly*) Since he was not able to pay, the
              master ordered that he and his wife and his
              children and all that he had be sold to repay the
              debt.
SERVANT 1:   (*Falls to knees, begging*) The servant fell on his
              knees before him. 'Be patient with me,' he
              begged, 'and I will pay back everything.'
MASTER: (*Pause*) The servant's master took pity on him,
              cancelled the debt and let him go.

(MASTER *freezes,* SERVANT 1 *looks visibly relieved.*)

JESUS: (*Disdainfully*) But when that servant went out,
              he found one of his fellow-servants who owed
              him a hundred denarii.

(JESUS *turns* SERVANT 1 *to face* SERVANT 2.)

He grabbed him and began to choke him. (*Act this out briefly and soberly!*)

SERVANT 1:   Pay back what you owe me!

SERVANT 2:   (*Falls to knees, begging*) His fellow-servant fell to his knees and begged him, 'Be patient with me, and I will pay you back.'

JESUS: But he refused.

(JESUS *swings* SERVANT 2 *round, who falls to his knees again at the rear of the stage, his back to the audience, head hung low.*)

JESUS: Instead, he went off and had the man thrown into prison until he could pay the debt. When the other servants saw what had happened, they were greatly distressed

(SERVANT 2 *whispers into the ear of the* MASTER.)

JESUS: and went and told their master everything that had happened.

MASTER: (*Annoyed*) Then the master called the servant in.

(SERVANT 1 *once more set face to face with* MASTER.)

MASTER: You wicked servant. I cancelled all that debt of yours because you begged me to. Shouldn't you have had mercy on your fellow-servant just as I had on you?

JESUS: In anger his master turned him over to the jailers to be tortured, until he should pay back all he owed.

(JESUS *swings* SERVANT 1 *around, who falls to his knees at rear of stage alongside* SERVANT 2. JESUS *then returns to his original seat and addresses concluding comment to* PETER.)

JESUS: This is how my heavenly Father will treat each of you unless you forgive your brother from your heart.

(*Opening music repeated as all exit.*)

NOTES

It is important that the characters not directly involved at any particular time in this reading remain totally still, so that the audience's concentration is correctly focused.

27. The Triumphal Entry

IN A NUTSHELL

The crowd or herd mentality is incredibly powerful, and it has always fascinated me how this same group of individuals could be as central at the triumphal entry as during the crucifixion. Reading two passages together where the crowd have totally opposite roles can easily highlight this. This passage in Matthew 21 shows the crowd in its most positive light.

Jesus' glory is obvious as the crowd raucously welcome his arrival in Jerusalem. Later on a change of temperature and a political upheaval alter their tune. Holding a freeze at the end of this reading with some suitable music can have the effect of hinting at what is to come.

Cast: NARRATOR, CROWD ENSEMBLE (4–8 people).

Props: Sound FX: crowd noise; music. Lights.

THE READING

(*Sound FX: crowd noise. Using a low light if possible, have silent ensemble as the* CROWD, *miming in slow motion – cheering, waving, throwing things, whistling, etc. The crowd noise slowly dies and is replaced by music. The* CROWD *freeze. Music slowly fades as* NARRATOR *begins.*)

NARR: (*Clearly and steadily*) As they approached Jerusalem and came to Bethphage on the Mount of Olives, Jesus sent two disciples,

143

saying to them, 'Go to the village ahead of you, and at once you will find a donkey tied there, with her colt by her. Untie them and bring them to me. If anyone says anything to you, tell him that the Lord needs them, and he will send them right away.'

This took place to fulfil what was spoken through the prophet: 'Say to the Daughter of Zion, "See, your king comes to you, gentle and riding on a donkey, on a colt, the foal of a donkey."'

The disciples went and did as Jesus had instructed them. They brought the donkey and the colt, placed their cloaks on them, and Jesus sat on them.

(*Mixture of music and crowd noises is brought up again.* CROWD *continue a variety of slow-motion movements relating to the following text.*)

A very large crowd spread their cloaks on the road, while others cut branches from the trees and spread them on the road. The crowds that went ahead of him and those that followed shouted,

(NARRATOR *speaks the words.* ENSEMBLE *can mime parts of the text, but not together and not in time with the* NARRATOR. *Remember the* ENSEMBLE *are miming in slow motion, so the words should be spoken at a slower speed. Set the background noise a bit higher for this next sequence, but not so loud that the audience can't hear the* NARRATOR.)

(*With raised voice*) 'Hosanna to the Son of David!'

'Blessed is he who comes in the name of the Lord!'

'Hosanna in the highest!'

(Volume lowers again as CROWD *talk among themselves. During the final two verses,* CROWD *nudge each other and look at given point at back of hall, indicating that they have seen Jesus.)*

When Jesus entered Jerusalem, the whole city was stirred and asked, 'Who is this?' The crowds answered, 'This is Jesus, the prophet from Nazareth in Galilee.'

(CROWD *hold freeze, focused on the invisible Jesus with different expressions. Music and lights slowly fade.)*

NOTES

In rehearsal, try out sound levels and crowd movements to find the most effective balance with the narrator's words. You are trying to give the impression of an excited and deafeningly noisy crowd scene, while at the same time ensuring that your audience can hear every word of the story.

Together, this and the following five readings cover the basic elements of the passion sequence. Using various styles you could present them all together, spread out with other elements in an Easter service or presentation. Think of how you can link them creatively using music and lighting if available. One suggestion is to use excerpts from Bach's *St Matthew's Passion*.

28. The Lord's Supper

IN A NUTSHELL

The Passover conjures up the traditional image represented in classical art. The Last Supper was in fact the first supper, to be repeated countless times at Communion services all around the world. Jesus gave his disciples the message of victory over death and the arrival of the Holy Spirit, but, as is so often true, things had to get worse before they got better.

Take some time to read up on the relevance of the Passover, how it was celebrated and what it meant. For this reading, we only have Jesus and Judas seated at the table. The congregation will be willing to accept that the others are there courtesy of the text. This also helps us to avoid a cluttered stage and to focus our thoughts on the two most central characters in the passage.

Cast: NARRATOR, JESUS, JUDAS.

Props: Sound FX: opening music; party sounds – chatter, clinking glasses, etc.; hymn music. Long table. Chairs. Bowl of water. Bread. Cup.

THE READING

(*A long table.* JESUS *sits at one end,* JUDAS *at the other holding a bowl into which he occasionally dips his hand to drink water. Quiet music plays as this freeze-frame is set. Music fades.*)

146

NARR: On the first day of the Feast of Unleavened Bread, the disciples came to Jesus and asked, 'Where do you want us to make preparations for you to eat the Passover?'

He replied, 'Go into the city to a certain man and tell him, "The Teacher says: My appointed time is near. I am going to celebrate the Passover with my disciples at your house."'

So the disciples did as Jesus had directed them and prepared the Passover.

(Background sound FX of friends socialising, low chatter, clinking of plates and glasses, etc. At this point the freeze-frame is broken.)

When evening came, Jesus was reclining at the table with the Twelve. And while they were eating, he said,

JESUS: I tell you the truth, *(Pause)* one of you will betray me.

NARR: They were very sad and began to say to him one after the other, 'Surely not I, Lord?'

JESUS: *(Brief silence as* JESUS *stares at* JUDAS*)* The one who has dipped his hand into the bowl with me will betray me. The Son of Man will go just as it is written about him. But woe to that man who betrays the Son of Man! It would be better for him if he had not been born.

JUDAS: Then Judas, the one who would betray him, said, *(Pause)* 'Surely not I, Rabbi?'

JESUS: Yes, it is you.

(Pause as JESUS *and* JUDAS *look at one another, conveying a sense of disappointment and shame respectively. Sound FX of party brought back up, at which point* JUDAS *exits.)*

NARR: While they were eating, Jesus took bread, gave thanks and broke it, and gave it to his disciples, saying,

JESUS: (*Breaking bread*) Take and eat; this is my body.

NARR: Then he took the cup, gave thanks and offered it to them, saying,

JESUS: (*Raising cup*) Drink from it, all of you. This is my blood of the covenant, which is poured out for many for the forgiveness of sins. I tell you, I will not drink of this fruit of the vine from now on until that day when I drink it anew with you in my Father's kingdom.

NARR: When they had sung a hymn, they went out to the Mount of Olives.

(*Music or congregational hymn is played as* JESUS *exits.*)

29. Jesus Arrested

IN A NUTSHELL

Jesus was arrested at night, probably because in the daytime the baying crowds would have made the task impossible. The religious leaders were painfully aware of who Jesus was – he had caused them nothing but trouble since his arrival – but Judas still physically pointed him out, as he was the formal accuser. When presenting this reading, try to create a dark, cloak-and-dagger atmosphere with music, sound and light.

As for the last piece, I have only used Jesus and Judas here, leaving the rest to the audience's imagination and including them as the group coming to arrest Jesus.

Cast: NARRATOR, JESUS, JUDAS.

Props: Sound FX: background music. Lights.

THE READING

(*Lights up on* JESUS *standing frozen centre stage. He looks at peace, an innocent lamb awaiting slaughter. During the reading of verse 47* JUDAS *enters from the back of the church through the congregation, who in effect form the large crowd referred to in the text.*)

NARR: While he was still speaking, Judas, one of the Twelve, arrived. With him was a large crowd armed with swords and clubs, sent from the

	chief priests and the elders of the people. Now the betrayer had arranged a signal with them:
JUDAS:	(*Aside to audience*) The one I kiss is the man; arrest him. (*Approaching* JESUS) Going at once to Jesus, Judas said, 'Greetings, Rabbi!' and kissed him. (JUDAS *steps close to* JESUS *to greet and kiss him*)
JESUS:	Friend, do what you came for.
NARR:	(*Pause*) Then the men stepped forward, seized Jesus and arrested him.

(JUDAS *becomes one of the crowd, steps behind* JESUS *and secures his arms.*)

	(*With urgency in voice*) With that, one of Jesus' companions reached for his sword, drew it out and struck the servant of the high priest, cutting off his ear.
JESUS:	Put your sword back in its place, for all who draw the sword will die by the sword. Do you think I cannot call on my Father, and he will at once put at my disposal more than twelve legions of angels? But how then would the Scriptures be fulfilled that say it must happen in this way?

(*Music plays quietly and continues underneath rest of the text.*)

NARR:	At that time Jesus said to the crowd,

(JUDAS *lets go of* JESUS.)

JESUS:	(*Plea to the crowd*) Am I leading a rebellion, that you have come out with swords and clubs

to capture me? Every day I sat in the temple courts teaching, and you did not arrest me. But this has all taken place that the writings of the prophets might be fulfilled.

(JESUS *freely holds out his arms and once again* JUDAS *secures him.* JUDAS *then leads* JESUS *slowly offstage.*)

NARR: Then all the disciples deserted him and fled.

(*Music slowly fades as* JUDAS *and* JESUS *complete their exit.*)

30. Jesus Before Pilate

IN A NUTSHELL

The passion sequence now moves on to Jesus standing trial before Pilate. From a dramatic point of view, Pilate is one of the most interesting supporting characters in the story. Not only is he multilayered, but it is also easy to imagine him functioning today in the back-stabbing political arena. Did Pilate want to crucify Jesus? No, not really – which may give us some ground for sympathy. Was he willing to crucify Jesus for popularity and political gain? Absolutely – which shows us the gaping weakness in his character. He felt the weight of pressure from religious authorities and political allies, the fervent crowd and even his own wife!

Imagine the scene as Jesus was brought before the all-powerful governor. Roles were completely reversed, with the accused standing totally calm and the judge a sweating bundle of nerves. When dramatising this scene, Jesus should remain in serene stillness, with Pilate constantly moving – striding around the accused. I have scripted this for a narrator, plus Jesus and Pilate. You will need a few people in non-speaking roles to play Barabbas and other general security guards. The congregation is again the crowd.

Cast: NARRATOR, JESUS, PILATE, plus small ensemble of 2–4.

Props: Sound FX: music; unruly crowd noises, including shouts of 'Crucify him!' Bowl of water.

THE READING

(*Music plays as guards lead in* JESUS. *He stands totally still centre stage. Guards stand a few feet on either side of him. They wait as music fades.*)

NARR:	Jesus stood before the governor, and the governor asked him,
PILATE:	(*Enters, agitated*) Are you the king of the Jews?
JESUS:	(*Pause*) Yes, it is as you say.
NARR:	When he was accused by the chief priests and the elders, he gave no answer. Then Pilate asked him,
PILATE:	Don't you hear the testimony they are bringing against you? (*Walks around* JESUS *in despair*)
NARR:	But Jesus made no reply, not even to a single charge – to the great amazement of the governor.
	Now it was the governor's custom at the Feast to release a prisoner chosen by the crowd. At that time they had a notorious prisoner, called Barabbas.

(*Member of the ensemble steps forward to represent Barabbas.*)

	So when the crowd had gathered, Pilate asked them,
PILATE:	(*To congregation*) Which one do you want me to release to you: Barabbas, (PILATE *gestures towards him*) or Jesus who is called Christ?

(*Guard shoves* JESUS *to opposite side of* PILATE *from Barabbas.*)

NARR:	(*Aside to audience*) For he knew it was out of envy that they had handed Jesus over to him.

While Pilate was sitting on the judge's seat, his wife sent him this message: (*As nagging wife*) 'Don't have anything to do with that innocent man, for I have suffered a great deal today in a dream because of him.'

But the chief priests and the elders persuaded the crowd to ask for Barabbas and to have Jesus executed.

PILATE: (*Impatiently to the congregation*) Which of the two do you want me to release to you?

NARR: 'Barabbas,' they answered.

PILATE: (*Nervously*) What shall I do, then, with Jesus who is called Christ?

NARR: They all answered, 'Crucify him!'

PILATE: (*Pause*) Why? What crime has he committed?

NARR: But they shouted all the louder, 'Crucify him!'

(*Sound FX of unruly crowd. Cries of 'Crucify him!' After about ten seconds* PILATE *holds up his hands and claps. Silence. A member of the ensemble brings a bowl of water and kneels in front of* PILATE *holding it up.*)

When Pilate saw that he was getting nowhere, but that instead an uproar was starting, he took water and washed his hands in front of the crowd.

PILATE: (*Washing hands*) I am innocent of this man's blood. It is your responsibility!

NARR: All the people answered, 'Let his blood be on us and on our children!' (*Pause*) Then he released Barabbas to them.

(PILATE *reluctantly nods to Barabbas, who smiles and walks into congregation.*)

But he had Jesus flogged, and handed him over to be crucified.

(*Laden with guilt,* PILATE *nods to* JESUS, *who is led away by guards. Music plays. All exit except* PILATE, *who looks into the distance for a few seconds, then strides off purposefully . Music fades.*)

31. The Crucifixion and Death of Jesus

IN A NUTSHELL

In performance there is no more powerful image than that of the cross. Whether your audience is Christian or not, that symbol, however basically it is portrayed, has the ability to touch hearts and minds in a very profound way. For this reading I have not scripted a physical crucified Jesus, but, as with the 'triumphal entry' reading, I have viewed the events from the crowd's perspective.

Imagine what it would have been like to be part of the crowd on that day, witnessing Christ carrying his cross, suffering mockery and the physical horror of crucifixion, and perhaps even hearing some of his final words. As the individuals threw their insults, were they meant from the heart, or were they just acting in solidarity with the rest of the crowd? Did the crowd have any perception that the act which was unfolding before them had such huge personal relevance to them?

This piece has been written as a narration with an ensemble of four taking certain lines and creating various images. With a bit of rehearsal, the effect should be very powerful.

Cast: NARRATOR, ENSEMBLE (4 people).

Props: Sound FX: opening music; six drum beats; raucous music; solemn music; earthquake and thunder. Lighting. Scarlet robe, crown of thorns, two sticks. Cross (prop or visual image). Bottle. Dice. Sign reading 'This is Jesus, the King of the Jews'. Sponge on a stick.

THE READING

(*Opening music.* ENSEMBLE *enter and stand in a square with their backs to the congregation. If possible the lighting should be low.*)

NARR: Then the governor's soldiers took Jesus into the Praetorium and gathered the whole company of soldiers round him. They stripped him and put a scarlet robe on him,

(ONE *holds up high a robe dangled on a stick.*)

and then twisted together a crown of thorns and set it on his head.

(TWO *holds up a crown of thorns hung on a stick.*)

They put a staff in his right hand and knelt in front of him and mocked him.

THREE/FOUR: (*Kneeling and mocking*) Hail, king of the Jews!

NARR: They spat on him, and took the staff and struck him on the head again and again.

(ONE *and* TWO *bring down their sticks in slow motion; a drum is beaten six times.*)

After they had mocked him, they took off the robe and put his own clothes on him. Then they led him away to crucify him.

(*Music plays as an image of the cross appears. This can be created using a prop, projection or any suitable visual image.* ENSEMBLE *stand frozen, looking at cross.*)

As they were going out, they met a man from Cyrene, named Simon, and they forced him to carry the cross. They came to a place called Golgotha (which means The Place of the Skull). There they offered Jesus wine to drink, mixed with gall;

(ONE *offers up a bottle*.)

but after tasting it, he refused to drink it.

(ENSEMBLE *laugh and there begins raucous music. They start to play a game of dice.*)

When they had crucified him, they divided up his clothes by casting lots.

(*The winner of the game proudly holds aloft Jesus' robe. They all collapse to the floor.*)

And sitting down, they kept watch over him there. Above his head they placed the written charge against him:

(THREE *holds up a written sign, the others laugh.*)

THIS IS JESUS, THE KING OF THE JEWS. Two robbers were crucified with him, one on his right and one on his left. Those who passed by hurled insults at him, shaking their heads and saying,

ONE: You who are going to destroy the temple and build it in three days, save yourself!

TWO: Come down from the cross, if you are the Son of God!

NARR: In the same way the chief priests, the teachers
          of the law and the elders mocked him.
THREE: He saved others, but he can't save himself!
FOUR: He's the King of Israel! Let him come down
          now from the cross, and we will believe in him.
THREE: (*Sarcastic*) He trusts in God. Let God rescue
          him now if he wants him, for he said, 'I am the
          Son of God.'

(*They all laugh.*)

NARR: In the same way the robbers who were crucified
          with him also heaped insults on him.

(*Solemn music.* ENSEMBLE *resume opening positions as the
lights slowly dim.*)

          From the sixth hour until the ninth hour
          darkness came over all the land. About the
          ninth hour Jesus cried out in a loud voice,
          '*Eloi, Eloi, lama sabachthani?*' – which means,
          'My God, my God, why have you forsaken
          me?'
          When some of those standing there heard
          this, they said, 'He's calling Elijah.' Immedi-
          ately one of them ran and got a sponge. He
          filled it with wine vinegar, put it on a stick, and
          offered it to Jesus to drink.

(ONE *offers up sponge on a stick.*)

TWO: Now leave him alone. Let's see if Elijah comes
          to save him.

(ENSEMBLE *slowly exit.*)

NARR: And when Jesus had cried out again in a loud
voice, he gave up his spirit. At that moment the
curtain of the temple was torn in two from top
to bottom. The earth shook and the rocks split.

(*Lights fade to blackout. Sound FX: earthquake and thunder.*)

MATTHEW 28:1–10

32. The Resurrection

IN A NUTSHELL

In a series of readings covering the passion of Jesus, it would be ridiculous to leave him on the cross, so we now turn to news of his resurrection. Unfortunately, this element of the life of Christ has been put under a magnifying glass and shrouded with controversy. I believe in its physical truth, in its message that Jesus is the Son of God with power over death. To believe this hardly stretches our faith: if we believe in a God who can create the world, surely we can believe that he is able to resurrect his Son!

Imagine the two Marys being first on the scene, hearing the angel speak the words that form the central pin of the passage: Jesus is not here, come and see for yourself, he is alive; now go and tell the disciples. As if this wasn't shock enough, a little later on they come face to face with the risen Jesus.

I have scripted this passage very simply, using two voices – a narrator and a second reader to speak the words of the angel and Jesus.

Cast: NARRATOR, READER (to play ANGEL and JESUS).

Props: Sound FX: dawn chorus.

THE READING

(*Sound FX: dawn chorus. Two readers simply stand to read.*)

161

NARR: After the Sabbath, at dawn on the first day of the week, Mary Magdalene and the other Mary went to look at the tomb.

There was a violent earthquake, for an angel of the Lord came down from heaven and, going to the tomb, rolled back the stone and sat on it. (*Quietly and awestruck*) His appearance was like lightning, and his clothes were as white as snow. (*Faster to indicate fear*) The guards were so afraid of him that they shook and became like dead men. The angel said to the women,

ANGEL: (*Calming but not hypnotic*) Do not be afraid, for I know that you are looking for Jesus, who was crucified. He is not here; he has risen, just as he said.

Come and see the place where he lay. Then go quickly and tell the disciples: 'He has risen from the dead and is going ahead of you into Galilee. There you will see him.' Now I have told you.

NARR: (*Pause*) So the women hurried away from the tomb, afraid yet filled with joy, and ran to tell his disciples. Suddenly Jesus met them.

JESUS: Greetings.

NARR: (*Reverently*) They came to him, clasped his feet and worshipped him. Then Jesus said to them,

JESUS: (*Pause, smiling*) Do not be afraid. Go and tell my brothers to go to Galilee; there they will see me.

33. Jesus Feeds the Five Thousand

IN A NUTSHELL

We may live in a place and time in which Christianity is regularly mocked, and people know little to nothing about the claims of Christ, but even so, few have not heard about the miracle of the loaves and fishes. How can we breathe new life into this old story?

Read the preceding chapter, and you can surmise Jesus' state of mind. John the Baptist has been murdered and Jesus is obviously bereaved. He and his apostles are in need of some rest and try unsuccessfully to withdraw. The crowds follow and, in an act of compassion, Christ still ministers to them. It is easy to draw modern-day parallels about busy lives and individuals in the church heading fast towards total spiritual burnout, but it also shows this story to be more than a miracle. We can also see a parable of incredible commitment, love and compassion.

I have scripted this using a narrator, Jesus and three disciples. The staging of it is very simple and attempts to add to the story a depiction of the tiredness and state of mind of the disciples and Jesus.

Cast: NARRATOR, JESUS, DISCIPLES (3).

Props: Sound FX: solemn music. Carrier bag containing bread and fish.

THE READING

(*Solemn music.* JESUS *stands stage left, surrounded by three* DISCIPLES. *They look tired but defiant, deflated by the news of John the Baptist's death.*)

NARR: The apostles gathered round Jesus and reported to him all they had done and taught. Then, because so many people were coming and going that they did not even have a chance to eat, he said to them,

JESUS: Come with me by yourselves to a quiet place and get some rest.

(JESUS *slowly turns and walks in a semicircle around the stage to the other side, followed by the* DISCIPLES. *This happens during the reading of verses 32–34.*)

NARR: So they went away by themselves in a boat to a solitary place. But many who saw them leaving recognised them and ran on foot from all the towns and got there ahead of them.

When Jesus landed and saw a large crowd, he had compassion on them, because they were like sheep without a shepherd. So he began teaching them many things. By this time it was late in the day, so his disciples came to him.

ONE: (*Irritated*) This is a remote place, and it's already very late. Send the people away so that they can go to the surrounding countryside and villages and buy themselves something to eat.

JESUS: You give them something to eat.

TWO: (*Smiling*) That would take eight months of a man's wages! Are we to go and spend that much on bread and give it to them to eat?

JESUS: (*Pause*) How many loaves do you have?

(TWO *looks at him blankly and shrugs his shoulders.*)

                  (*Impatiently*) Go and see.
NARR: When they found out, they said,
THREE: (*Holding carrier bag with bread and fish in it*)
                  Five – (*Pause*) and two fish.
NARR: Then Jesus directed them to have all the people
                  sit down in groups on the green grass.

(*The* DISCIPLES *sit on the floor, scattered around stage.*)

                  So they sat down in groups of hundreds and
                  fifties. Taking the five loaves and the two fish
                  and looking up to heaven, he gave thanks and
                  broke the loaves.

(JESUS *breaks bread.*)

                  Then he gave them to his disciples to set before
                  the people.

(JESUS *hands bread out to* DISCIPLES *while reading continues.
As the* DISCIPLES *receive, they exit as if about to hand out to
congregated crowds.*)

                  He also divided the two fish among them all.
                  They all ate and were satisfied, and the disciples
                  picked up twelve basketfuls of broken pieces of
                  bread and fish. The number of men who had
                  eaten was five thousand.

(*By the time the narration has finished,* JESUS *and* DISCIPLES
should all have left the stage.)

34. The Parable of the Good Samaritan

IN A NUTSHELL

As with so many readings in this collection, it can be of a distinct advantage to be communicating something that is familiar to the listener, although it gives us the difficulty of finding an original method. I have written sketches that put various spins on this story, but here I have scripted the passage with some interaction while relying heavily on a powerful piece of storytelling by the reader playing Jesus.

When preparing the reading, look at the characters involved and try to understand what prompted their actions. Imagine the tension between Jews and Samaritans; what modern-day parallel can be drawn to increase understanding? A good half of this reading is a monologue by Jesus. It is therefore essential that the reader pictures the story as he tells it, using facial expressions and vocal changes to communicate.

Cast: JESUS, MAN.

Props: Two chairs. File. Two silver coins.

THE READING

(JESUS *is seated, relaxing with his eyes closed.* MAN *is frantically flicking through a file. He finds something and smiles before addressing audience.*)

166

MAN: On one occasion an expert in the law stood up to test Jesus. (*Stands to address* JESUS) 'Teacher, what must I do to inherit eternal life?'

JESUS: (*Gestures to man's file*) What is written in the Law? How do you read it?

MAN: (*Trots off reply by rote, with no feeling*) 'Love the Lord your God with all your heart and with all your soul and with all your strength and with all your mind'; and, 'Love your neighbour as yourself.'

JESUS: (*Pause for thought*) You have answered correctly. Do this and you will live. (*Closes his eyes again, indicating end of conversation*)

MAN: (*Pause, aside to audience*) But he wanted to justify himself, so he asked Jesus, (*Turns to* JESUS) 'And who is my neighbour?'

(JESUS *smiles, deciding to give* MAN *the full answer. He indicates for* MAN *to sit down, which he does.* JESUS *tells story* Jackanory *style.*)

JESUS: A man was going down from Jerusalem to Jericho, when he fell into the hands of robbers. They stripped him of his clothes, beat him and went away, leaving him half-dead.

A priest happened to be going down the same road, and when he saw the man, he passed by on the other side.

So too, a Levite, when he came to the place and saw him, passed by on the other side.

But (*Pause*) a Samaritan, as he travelled, came where the man was; and when he saw him, he took pity on him. He went to him and bandaged his wounds, pouring on oil and wine. Then he put the man on his own donkey, brought him to an inn and took care of him.

The next day he took out two silver coins and gave them to the innkeeper. (*Takes out two coins and spins them over to* MAN) 'Look after him,' he said, 'and when I return, I will reimburse you for any extra expense you may have.'

(*Holds out hands to indicate end of story*) Which of these three do you think was a neighbour to the man who fell into the hands of robbers?

MAN: The one who had mercy on him.

JESUS: (*Pause, smiling*) Go and do likewise.

(MAN *gathers file and exits.* JESUS, *still smiling, shuts his eyes again. Lights fade.*)

NOTES

The key to an effective reading of this passage is in the element of storytelling. A good model to bear in mind is the BBC show *Jackanory*, on which various actors read children's stories, accompanied by just a few illustrations. The challenge here is to create a vivid picture for the listener using only voice, expression, minimal movement and gesture.

Jesus was a master storyteller, drawing vast crowds when he spoke. The love and belief he had in what he was saying proved infectious, and that is the quality we must try to emulate.

LUKE 11:1–13

35. Jesus' Teaching on Prayer

IN A NUTSHELL

In this passage, the Lord's Prayer is a shortened version of the one we commonly use. Jesus then moves on to illustrate persistence in prayer, and finishes by showing how much the Father loves us. It is worth remembering these key points when delivering the reading.

In this script for three readers, I have attempted to illustrate Jesus' passion for prayer and right relationship with God by using his love of storytelling.

Cast: JESUS, ONE, TWO.

Props: Small toy snake.

THE READING

(ONE *and* TWO *sit either side of stage, facing front and looking into space.* JESUS *is kneeling centre stage at the rear.*)

JESUS:	One day Jesus was praying in a certain place. When he finished, (*Stands up and awaits attention of disciples, which is not forthcoming. He clears his throat, which stirs them into action*) one of his disciples said to him,
ONE:	Lord, teach us to pray, just as John taught his disciples.
JESUS:	When you pray, say: (*Pause, then with sincere devotion*) 'Father, hallowed be your name, your kingdom come. (*Pause*)

169

'Give us each day our daily bread. Forgive us our sins, for we also forgive everyone who sins against us. And lead us not into temptation.'

(*Changes to excited storytelling mode. He moves the disciples into position for the story.*)

	Suppose one of you has a friend, and he goes to him at midnight and says,
ONE:	(*Becoming character in story*) Friend, lend me three loaves of bread, because a friend of mine on a journey has come to me, and I have nothing to set before him.
JESUS:	Then the one inside answers him, (JESUS *indicates for* TWO *to play the role*)
TWO:	(*Becomes other frustrated friend*) Don't bother me. The door is already locked, and my children are with me in bed. I can't get up and give you anything.
JESUS:	I tell you, though he will not get up and give him the bread because he is his friend, yet because of the man's boldness he will get up and give him as much as he needs.

(*Seriously*) So I say to you: Ask and it will be given to you; seek and you will find; knock and the door will be opened to you. For everyone who asks receives; he who seeks finds; and to him who knocks, the door will be opened.

(ONE *and* TWO *look thoroughly confused.* JESUS *continues.*)

(*As if to explain*) Which of you fathers, if your son asks for a fish, will give him a snake instead?

(*Takes* ONE*'s hand and puts a small toy snake in it, which has been concealed in clothing.* ONE *jumps and throws snake off-stage.*)

(*Turns to* TWO) Or if he asks for an egg, will give him a scorpion?

(TWO *looks worried, but* JESUS *smiles and shakes his head as if to say, 'I wouldn't be that cruel!'*)

If you then, though you are evil, know how to give good gifts to your children, how much more will your Father in heaven give the Holy Spirit to those who ask him!

36. The Parable of the Lost Son

IN A NUTSHELL

To understand the parable of the lost son fully, we need to have a basic understanding of the culture of the time. By asking for his share of the estate, the son was greatly disrespecting his father's authority and position. The way he spent the money showed even more disrespect. As if his new lifestyle wasn't degrading enough, he then resorted to feeding pigs, when for a Jew a pig was an unclean animal not even to be touched!

Even though the son had wandered purposely from his father, he was willing to accept him back, in the same way that God is prepared to reach out to all sinners. I love the fact that the father runs to greet his son. In that culture an older man would normally have walked with dignity, but such is his delight to see his son, he hitches up his long garment and runs to meet him.

If I'm honest, I've always had a bit of a soft spot for the much maligned older brother. His response, though wrong, is understandable. We are not so much comparing the two brothers' actions, but rather the responses of the father and older brother to the younger brother's action. If we become too self-righteous, aware of others' faults and conveniently unaware of our own, we become like the Pharisees of old.

For this piece I have used the more traditional method of miming to a narration – with a few interesting little flourishes!

Cast: NARRATOR, FATHER, SON 1, SON 2, SERVANT, ENSEMBLE of 2–4.

Props: Sound FX: opening music (on theme of fathers, sons or brothers); *Chariots of Fire* theme tune. Desk and chair. Three moneybags and some coins. Signs reading 'Distant country' and 'Fattened calf'.

THE READING

(*Opening music.* FATHER *is sitting at desk counting money – there are three bags on desk.*)

NARR: Jesus continued: There was a man who had two sons. The younger one said to his father,

SON 1: Father, give me my share of the estate.

(FATHER *pauses for thought, then throws him one of the moneybags.*)

NARR: So he divided his property between them. Not long after that, the younger son got together all he had, set off for a distant country

(*One of the* ENSEMBLE *holds up sign reading 'Distant country'.*)

and there squandered his wealth in wild living.

(ENSEMBLE *mime scene of wild living. Be creative here in portraying music, dancing, women, drugs, gambling, etc. Try out a few ideas, choosing the best, but keep it punchy.*)

After he had spent everything, there was a severe famine in that whole country, and he began to be in need.

(SON 1 *is left alone on stage in desperation. Money is gone, and possessions, even the coat from his back.*)

So he went and hired himself out to a citizen of that country, who sent him to his fields to feed pigs.

(*Two of* ENSEMBLE *become pigs and* SON 1 *feeds them. Minimal snorting is optional!*)

He longed to fill his stomach with the pods that the pigs were eating, but no-one gave him anything.

(SON 1 *sinks to his knees; the pigs look a bit put out.*)

When he came to his senses, he said,

SON 1:   How many of my father's hired men have food to spare, and here I am starving to death! I will set out and go back to my father and say to him: (*As if practising a big speech*) Father, I have sinned against heaven and against you. I am no longer worthy to be called your son; make me like one of your hired men.

(*Pigs nod and snort their agreement and walk off.*)

NARR: So he got up and went to his father. But while he was still a long way off, his father saw him and was filled with compassion for him; he ran to his son, threw his arms around him and kissed him.

(FATHER *runs in slow motion towards* SON 1 *and they embrace, accompanied by the* Chariots of Fire *theme tune.*)

SON 1:   Father, I have sinned against heaven and against you. I am no longer worthy to be called your son.

NARR: But the father said to his servants,

FATHER: (*Excited*) Quick! Bring the best robe and put it on him. Put a ring on his finger and sandals on his feet. Bring the fattened calf and kill it.

(*Member of* ENSEMBLE *appears at rear of stage wearing a sign around his neck reading 'Fattened calf'. At mention of his name, he looks panic stricken and tiptoes offstage.*)

             Let's have a feast and celebrate. For this son of mine was dead and is alive again; he was lost and is found.

NARR: So they began to celebrate. (*Short cheer of celebration*) Meanwhile, the older son was in the field.

(SON 2 *stands at side of stage.*)

             When he came near the house, he heard music and dancing. So he called one of the servants and asked him what was going on.

SERVANT: (*Comes over to* SON 2) Your brother has come, and your father has killed the fattened calf because he has him back safe and sound.

(*Two of* ENSEMBLE *carry fattened calf across back of stage.* SERVANT *and* SON 2 *watch.*)

NARR: The older brother became angry and refused to go in. So his father went out and pleaded with him.

(FATHER *goes to* SON 2.)

             But he answered his father,

SON 2:   (*As moody teenager*) Look! All these years I've been slaving for you and never disobeyed your orders. Yet you never gave me even a young goat so I could celebrate with my friends. But when this son of yours who has squandered your property with prostitutes comes home, you kill the fattened calf for him!

FATHER: My son, you are always with me, and everything I have is yours. But we had to celebrate and be glad, because this brother of yours was dead and is alive again; he was lost and is found.

(*They exit.*)

NOTES

Humour is a great tool for communication, but needs to be used wisely. In a family service or youth event, for instance, this style works well, but if you are reading at a more worship-orientated Communion service, it is wiser to hold back.

37. Zacchaeus the Tax Collector

IN A NUTSHELL

The Jews really hated paying the taxes levied by the Romans, especially when corrupt tax collectors were creaming extra off the top for their own pockets. Although tax always plays a big role in our general elections, and the tax office is not seen as the most philanthropic of vocations, in this story the tax collectors were seen much more as outcasts of society. Make no mistake, Zacchaeus was not a popular man!

The story teaches us how an inward change should yield outward results. Faith should lead to action, which in this case it certainly did. The crowd may have found it difficult to understand that Zacchaeus was acceptable to Jesus, and we may find it difficult today to understand that people with different backgrounds or cultures are also acceptable, but that's just the way it is (thank God!).

Scripted for three performers and a narrator, this short piece is easy to put together and, with some basic, creative movement and props, should go down very well as an aperitif to the teaching.

Cast: NARRATOR, JESUS, ZACCHAEUS, CROWD (best played by one very tall and large man).

Props: Sound FX: crowd noise. Small stepladder. A couple of branches. Table and two chairs. Tray of tea things.

THE READING

(*Sound FX: crowd noise.* CROWD *stands with arms crossed,* ZACCHAEUS *hidden behind.*)

NARR: Jesus entered Jericho and was passing through.
           A man was there by the name of Zacchaeus; he
           was a chief tax collector and was wealthy. He
           wanted to see who Jesus was, but being a short
           man he could not, because of the crowd.

(ZACCHAEUS *desperately tries to see around* CROWD – *above, to sides, between legs – but* CROWD *always blocks his view.*)

           So he ran ahead and climbed a sycamore-fig
           tree to see him, since Jesus was coming that way.

(ZACCHAEUS *goes to side of stage where there is a small step-ladder with a couple of branches sticking out of it. He climbs it and holds branches to face, peeking through them.*)

           When Jesus reached the spot, he looked up and
           said to him,
JESUS: (*Enters and stares in shock at the idiotic-looking*
           ZACCHAEUS) Zacchaeus, come down immedi-
           ately. I must stay at your house today.
NARR: So he came down at once and welcomed him
           gladly.

(ZACCHAEUS *goes to* JESUS *and leads him to his house, signified by a table and two chairs.*)

           All the people saw this and began to mutter,
CROWD: (*Disapproving*) He has gone to be the guest of a
           'sinner'.

ZACC: (*Carrying in tray of tea*) But Zacchaeus stood up and said to the Lord, 'Look, Lord! Here and now I give half of my possessions to the poor, and if I have cheated anybody out of anything, I will pay back four times the amount.'

JESUS: (*Gestures for* ZACCHAEUS *to sit, which he does*) Today salvation has come to this house, because this man, too, is a son of Abraham. For the Son of Man came to seek and to save what was lost.

(ZACCHAEUS *smiles and offers* JESUS *tea.*)

NOTES

In this piece I have given a very odd prop suggestion: a tree made from a stepladder and a couple of branches! You may think it sounds a bit naff, but I love creative and minimalist props that are a bit odd, and as a rule audiences do too. It will be totally obvious that it signifies a tree, and having a man hold up two branches and peer through them furtively is, for some reason, a very funny image. The lesson we can draw from this is that sometimes less is more. We don't always need expensive sets and decoration – just a slice of creative imagination.

38. Jesus Changes Water to Wine

IN A NUTSHELL

Moving into the last of the Gospels, I have chosen the account of Jesus' famous first miracle of changing water into wine. Before Jesus began his mission, he was a guest at a wedding. The wedding would have lasted a week and often the whole town was invited. The huge social faux pas of running out of wine was very embarrassing, and Jesus (against his wishes, but with true compassion) saved the situation. Jesus changed the water into the best wine, just as he can change us into the best people we can be. There was over 100 gallons of it! Life for him would never be the same again. The people were amazed, and so were the disciples.

I've always wondered what it would have been like to be a servant at this wedding – just getting ready to go home, only to be launched back into work with a seemingly never-ending supply of wine. I suppose Jesus' miracles were never greeted with universal approval.

I have chosen to script this with a servant narrating the events, supported by an ensemble cast.

Cast: NARRATOR, JESUS, MARY, MASTER, ENSEMBLE of 2–4.

Props: Sound FX: wedding music. Empty wine bottle. Glass of red wine.

THE READING

(Wedding music is played. ENSEMBLE *form party onstage.* NAR-RATOR *steps forward to speak, but music is too loud. He gives signal for music to be cut, which it is, suddenly.)*

NARR:	On the third day a wedding took place at Cana in Galilee. Jesus' mother was there, *(Indicates her)* and Jesus and his disciples had also been invited to the wedding. *(Indicates them)* When the wine was gone, *(Upturns an empty bottle)* Jesus' mother said to him,
MARY:	They have no more wine.
JESUS:	*(Troubled)* Dear woman, why do you involve me? My time has not yet come.
NARR:	His mother said to the servants,
MARY:	*(To* NARRATOR, *excited and completely ignoring* JESUS' *plea)* Do whatever he tells you.
NARR:	Nearby stood six stone water jars, the kind used by the Jews for ceremonial washing, each holding from twenty to thirty gallons. Jesus said to the servants,
JESUS:	Fill the jars with water.
NARR:	So they filled them to the brim. *(Indicates to member of* ENSEMBLE *to obey command. They rush off)* Then he told them,
JESUS:	Now draw some out and take it to the master of the banquet.

(Member of ENSEMBLE *returns with a glass of red wine and hands it to* MASTER.*)*

NARR:	They did so, and the master of the banquet tasted the water that had been turned into wine. He did not realise where it had come from,

though the servants who had drawn the water knew.

(MASTER *tastes the wine very professionally.*)

MASTER: Then he called the bridegroom aside and said, Everyone brings out the choice wine first and then the cheaper wine after the guests have had too much to drink; (*With joy*) but you have saved the best till now. (*Swigs down rest of glass*)

NARR: This, the first of his miraculous signs, Jesus performed in Cana of Galilee. He thus revealed his glory, and his disciples put their faith in him.

(NARRATOR *clicks finger to indicate continuation of original music. All exit.*)

39. Jesus Teaches Nicodemus

IN A NUTSHELL

The next two readings focus on key verses and words that Jesus spoke. For both I have scripted straight readings, with just two voices – one for Jesus, the second for all other characters. It is important truly to understand what is being said, enabling you to communicate it effectively.

In this passage from John 3, Jesus teaches a Pharisee called Nicodemus, who is searching for truth. He was certainly well educated, but what he needed to have was an open mind and heart. Jesus then gives us an early blueprint for evangelism. Although key events were yet to occur, Jesus speaks passionately of the need to be born again and the work of the Holy Spirit, and gives the gospel in a nutshell. We've heard it from teachers, pastors and evangelists, but just for a moment imagine hearing the gospel message from Jesus Christ himself!

As you prepare this reading, study each verse and ensure you have a full understanding. Not only will you be touched, however many times you've read it before, but you'll also be ready to move others very powerfully with Christ's inspirational words.

Cast: JESUS, NICODEMUS.

Props: None required.

THE READING

(Both readers simply stand to deliver their lines.)

NIC: Now there was a man of the Pharisees named
            Nicodemus, a member of the Jewish ruling
            council.
                He came to Jesus at night and said, 'Rabbi,
            we know you are a teacher who has come from
            God. For no-one could perform the miraculous
            signs you are doing if God were not with him.'

JESUS: I tell you the truth, no-one can see the kingdom
            of God unless he is born again.

NIC: (*Confused*) How can a man be born when he is
            old? Surely he cannot enter a second time into
            his mother's womb to be born!

JESUS: (*Smiles*) I tell you the truth, no-one can enter
            the kingdom of God unless he is born of water
            and the Spirit. Flesh gives birth to flesh, but the
            Spirit gives birth to spirit. You should not be
            surprised at my saying, 'You must be born
            again.'
                (*Slightly more animated*) The wind blows
            wherever it pleases. You hear its sound, but you
            cannot tell where it comes from or where it is
            going. So it is with everyone born of the Spirit.

NIC: (*Still confused, but keen to understand*) How can
            this be?

JESUS: (*Pause, then as if to explain*) You are Israel's
            teacher, and do you not understand these
            things? I tell you the truth, we speak of what
            we know, and we testify to what we have seen,
            but still you people do not accept our testi-
            mony.
                (*Disappointed*) I have spoken to you of

earthly things and you do not believe; how then will you believe if I speak of heavenly things?

(*Stating fact*) No-one has ever gone into heaven except the one who came from heaven – the Son of Man.

(*Passionately*) Just as Moses lifted up the snake in the desert, so the Son of Man must be lifted up, that everyone who believes in him may have eternal life.

(*Quietly*) For God so loved the world that he gave his one and only Son, that whoever believes in him shall not perish but have eternal life.

(*With love*) For God did not send his Son into the world to condemn the world, but to save the world through him. Whoever believes in him is not condemned, but whoever does not believe stands condemned already because he has not believed in the name of God's one and only Son.

(*Pause*) This is the verdict: Light has come into the world, but men loved darkness instead of light because their deeds were evil. Everyone who does evil hates the light, and will not come into the light for fear that his deeds will be exposed.

(*Lighter tones*) But whoever lives by the truth comes into the light, so that it may be seen plainly that what he has done has been done through God.

NOTES

Without wishing to state the absolutely obvious, prayer is a central part of the ministry of Scripture reading. I encourage you to pray as you seek understanding of the Scriptures during preparation, and also to pray before you read that God will breathe life into the words through his Holy Spirit and powerfully touch all who listen with an open heart.

40. Jesus the Christ?

IN A NUTSHELL

In this passage Jesus very openly lays down his claim that he is the Messiah, to a variety of reactions. Some thought he was good, others deceitful, still others demon possessed! Many were hostile towards him, while others chose to believe his messianic claims. The challenge to both reader and listener is, 'Who do you say I am?' Don't thoughtlessly disregard the claims, but look into them with an open mind and decide for yourself – the choice will have eternal consequences.

Like the last passage, this reading is for two voices: one for Jesus, the second taking all other parts. Not only is the message powerful, but it also contains a great evangelistic theme.

Cast: JESUS, READER.

Props: None required.

THE READING

(*Both readers simply stand to deliver their lines.*)

READER: At that point some of the people of Jerusalem began to ask, (*As gossiping crowd*) 'Isn't this the man they are trying to kill? Here he is, speaking publicly, and they are not saying a word to him. Have the authorities really concluded that he is the Christ?

187

(*Change of tone*) 'But we know where this man is from; when the Christ comes, no-one will know where he is from.'

JESUS: Then Jesus, still teaching in the temple courts, cried out, 'Yes, you know me, and you know where I am from. I am not here on my own, but he who sent me is true. You do not know him, but I know him because I am from him and he sent me.'

READER: (*Annoyed*) At this they tried to seize him, (*Pause, then calmly*) but no-one laid a hand on him, because his time had not yet come.

Still, many in the crowd put their faith in him. They said, (*Amazed*) 'When the Christ comes, will he do more miraculous signs than this man?'

(*Pause, conspiratorial*) The Pharisees heard the crowd whispering such things about him. Then the chief priests and the Pharisees sent temple guards to arrest him.

JESUS: I am with you for only a short time, and then I go to the one who sent me. You will look for me, but you will not find me; and where I am, you cannot come.

READER: (*Mocking*) The Jews said to one another, 'Where does this man intend to go that we cannot find him? Will he go where our people live scattered among the Greeks, and teach the Greeks?

'What did he mean when he said, (*Mimics*) "You will look for me, but you will not find me," and "Where I am you cannot come"?'

JESUS: On the last and greatest day of the Feast, Jesus stood and said in a loud voice, (*Preaching mode*) 'If anyone is thirsty, let him come to me and drink. Whoever believes in me, as the Scripture has said, streams of living water will flow from within him.'

READER: (*Audience aside*) By this he meant the Spirit, whom those who believed in him were later to receive. Up to that time the Spirit had not been given, since Jesus had not yet been glorified.

On hearing his words, some of the people said, (*Change vocals to express differing opinions*) 'Surely this man is the Prophet.' Others said, 'He is the Christ.'

Still others asked, 'How can the Christ come from Galilee? Does not the Scripture say that the Christ will come from David's family and from Bethlehem, the town where David lived?'

(*Rounding up*) Thus the people were divided because of Jesus. Some wanted to seize him, but no-one laid a hand on him.

41. Jesus Raises Lazarus from the Dead

IN A NUTSHELL

The story of Lazarus has much to teach, but in dramatic terms we can focus on two main themes. First, and most obvious, is the miracle of Jesus physically raising Lazarus from the dead. Second, there is the tale of his two sisters, Mary and Martha, and their differing reactions to a visit from Jesus. The image of Mary praying and Martha busying herself has been the subject of many sketches, usually at the expense of poor Martha.

Read back to the beginning of the chapter to get the full picture before our chosen selection begins. In this passage we have the famous shortest verse of the Bible, 'Jesus wept.' As Jesus grieves with his people, we see a humane, caring side to his nature, empathising with human loss. I also love the fact that Martha, often the brunt of a joke, is seen as a wonderful woman of faith.

This passage communicates most strongly as a dialogue and narration rather than being acted out. I have scripted it in radio play format, with four readers sharing the words.

Cast: NARRATOR, JESUS, MARY, MARTHA.

Props: Sound FX: funeral dirge.

THE READING

(*Opening music, some kind of funeral dirge. Readers enter and take positions.*)

190

NARR: (*Solemnly*) On his arrival, Jesus found that Lazarus had already been in the tomb for four days. Bethany was less than two miles from Jerusalem, and many Jews had come to Martha and Mary to comfort them in the loss of their brother.

When Martha heard that Jesus was coming, she went out to meet him, but Mary stayed at home.

MARTHA: Lord, if you had been here, my brother would not have died. But I know that even now God will give you whatever you ask.

JESUS: Your brother will rise again.

MARTHA: I know he will rise again in the resurrection at the last day.

JESUS: I am the resurrection and the life. He who believes in me will live, even though he dies; and whoever lives and believes in me will never die. (*Pause*) Do you believe this?

MARTHA: (*Sincerely*) Yes, Lord, I believe that you are the Christ, the Son of God, who was to come into the world.

NARR: And after she had said this, she went back and called her sister Mary aside.

MARTHA: (*Urgently*) The Teacher is here, and is asking for you.

NARR: When Mary heard this, she got up and quickly went to him. Now Jesus had not yet entered the village, but was still at the place where Martha had met him.

When the Jews who had been with Mary in the house, comforting her, noticed how quickly she got up and went out, they followed her, supposing she was going to the tomb to mourn there.

When Mary reached the place where Jesus

was and saw him, she fell at his feet and said,

MARY: (*Mourning*) Lord, if you had been here, my brother would not have died.

NARR: When Jesus saw her weeping, and the Jews who had come along with her also weeping, he was deeply moved in spirit and troubled.

JESUS: (*Quietly*) Where have you laid him?

NARR: 'Come and see, Lord,' they replied.

(*Pause*) Jesus wept. Then the Jews said, 'See how he loved him!'

(*Frustrated*) But some of them said, 'Could not he who opened the eyes of the blind man have kept this man from dying?'

Jesus, once more deeply moved, came to the tomb. It was a cave with a stone laid across the entrance.

JESUS: Take away the stone.

MARTHA: (*Shocked*) But Lord, by this time there is a bad odour, for he has been there four days.

JESUS: Did I not tell you that if you believed, you would see the glory of God?

NARR: So they took away the stone. Then Jesus looked up and said,

JESUS: Father, I thank you that you have heard me. I knew that you always hear me, but I said this for the benefit of the people standing here, that they may believe that you sent me.

NARR: When he had said this, Jesus called in a loud voice,

JESUS: Lazarus, come out!

NARR: (*Pause, then amazed*) The dead man came out, his hands and feet wrapped with strips of linen, and a cloth around his face. Jesus said to them,

JESUS: (*Joyfully*) Take off the grave clothes and let him go.

42. The Holy Spirit Comes at Pentecost

IN A NUTSHELL

Pentecost was one of the major annual feasts that the Jews celebrated. Also known as the Festival of Weeks, it was a time of thanksgiving for harvested crops.

Nowadays this passage is used as a great call for the supernatural gifts of the Spirit, and understandably so, given its content. This has, however, tainted it with an element of controversy and disagreement, depending on a specific church's dogma. What I love about this passage runs contrary to that potential division. It speaks of an inclusiveness, with Jews from many nations gathering to celebrate, witnessing this great miracle and listening to Peter's speech.

As the tongues of fire come down, representing speech and communicating the gospel, people of all nations are able to communicate with one another. God is bigger than our expectations; he can speak in incredible and dramatic ways, or in the still, small silence.

Using one reader, I have scripted this with a variety of suggested tones and some ideas for a few effects to support the spoken word.

Cast: READER.

Props: Sound FX: violent wind; crowd noise and laughter. Lights. Large scroll.

THE READING

READER: When the day of Pentecost came, they were all
together in one place. Suddenly a sound like the
blowing of a violent wind came from heaven
and filled the whole house where they were
sitting.

(*Sound FX: quick blast of violent wind.*)

They saw what seemed to be tongues of fire that
separated and came to rest on each of them. All
of them were filled with the Holy Spirit and
began to speak in other tongues as the Spirit
enabled them.

(*Sound FX: crowd noise, builds to a crescendo then suddenly
stops.*)

(*As if telling a story*) Now there were staying in
Jerusalem God-fearing Jews from every nation
under heaven. When they heard this sound, a
crowd came together in bewilderment, because
each one heard them speaking in his own language. Utterly amazed, they asked:

(*This section is rather a mouthful, so practise it carefully. Read
it with tones of building amazement and excitement at what is
happening.*)

'Are not all these men who are speaking
Galileans? Then how is it that each of us hears
in his own language? Parthians, Medes and
Elamites; residents of Mesopotamia, Judea
and Cappadocia, Pontus and Asia, Phrygia

and Pamphylia, Egypt and the parts of Libya
near Cyrene; visitors from Rome (both Jews
and converts to Judaism); Cretans and Arabs –
we hear them declaring the wonders of God in
our own tongues!'

Amazed and perplexed, they asked one
another, 'What does this mean?' (*Dismissive*)
Some, however, made fun of them and said,
'They have had too much wine.'

(*Sound FX: raise volume on crowd noises and laughter.*
READER *changes position to become Peter. He raises his hand
to speak and the crowd noise stops.*)

Then Peter stood up with the Eleven, raised his
voice and addressed the crowd: (*Pause*) Fellow
Jews and all of you who live in Jerusalem, let
me explain this to you; listen carefully to what
I say. (*With humour*) These men are not drunk,
as you suppose. It's only nine in the morning!
No, this is what was spoken by the prophet Joel:

(*Lighting change if possible, as Peter reads from large scroll.
Read slowly and with meaning.*)

In the last days, God says, I will pour out my
    Spirit on all people.
Your sons and daughters will prophesy,
your young men will see visions,
your old men will dream dreams.
Even on my servants, both men and women,
I will pour out my Spirit in those days, and they
    will prophesy.
I will show wonders in the heavens above
and signs on the earth below,

blood and fire and billows of smoke.
The sun will be turned to darkness
and the moon to blood
before the coming of the great and glorious day
    of the Lord.
And everyone who calls on the name of the
    Lord will be saved.

(Short pause as lights fade to blackout.)

43. Saul's Conversion

IN A NUTSHELL

Sometimes we have an expectation of the sort of person God can use to do his work – maybe a well spoken, middle-class individual fits the bill! Well, of course God can use such people, but he also throws the net a lot wider. Saul was a Jew so zealous that he would persecute and murder to stop the gospel from spreading. Armed with letters of authority to arrest, Saul was heading for the commercial city of Damascus, perhaps figuring that by stamping out Christianity on this key trade route he could halt its progress. At this point, enter God and a rather famous flash of light.

The key thing to communicate in this passage, as well as the obvious conversion, is how we react to people we might think are unsuitable for God's service. God can empower anyone he sees fit, a point which is perfectly illustrated in this passage. I've scripted it as a narration with two additional speaking parts.

Cast: NARRATOR, SAUL, ANANIAS (plus 2 non-speaking roles).

Props: Sound FX: music to indicate evil plotting. Handful of letters. Spotlight. Chair.

THE READING

(*Music plays, illustrating* SAUL*'s evil and calculated plans.* SAUL *stands centre stage, between* TWO COMPANIONS, *audibly* *muttering and laughing. They are looking through various letters, later to be described. Music fades as* NARRATOR *speaks.*)

NARR: Meanwhile, Saul was still breathing out murderous threats against the Lord's disciples. He went to the high priest and asked him for letters to the synagogues in Damascus, so that if he found any there who belonged to the Way, whether men or women, he might take them as prisoners to Jerusalem.

As he neared Damascus on his journey, suddenly a light from heaven flashed around him.

(*If possible, shine spotlight on* SAUL. *The most important thing is* SAUL'*s reaction, falling to his knees, dropping letters and clutching his eyes.*)

He fell to the ground and heard a voice say to him, (*Vocal change*) 'Saul, Saul, why do you persecute me?'

SAUL: (*In pain*) Who are you, Lord?

NARR: 'I am Jesus, whom you are persecuting,' he replied. 'Now get up and go into the city, and you will be told what you must do.'

(*Revert to original voice*) The men travelling with Saul stood there speechless; they heard the sound but did not see anyone.

(COMPANIONS *act out the text in a minimal way. They are confused, as they do not hear the voice, but also concerned for* SAUL. *They help him to his feet.*)

Saul got up from the ground, but when he opened his eyes he could see nothing. So they led him by the hand into Damascus. For three

days he was blind, and did not eat or drink anything.

(COMPANIONS *lead* SAUL *to a chair at side of stage. They leave*
him. ANANIAS *appears opposite side of stage, occupied with*
something like painting or reading.)

                (*Pause*) In Damascus there was a disciple
                named Ananias. The Lord called to him in a
                vision, 'Ananias!'

ANANIAS: (*Jumps*) Yes, Lord.

NARR: The Lord told him, 'Go to the house of Judas
                on Straight Street and ask for a man from
                Tarsus named Saul, for he is praying. In a
                vision he has seen a man named Ananias come
                and place his hands on him to restore his sight.'

ANANIAS: (*Reluctantly*) Lord, I have heard many reports
                about this man and all the harm he has done to
                your saints in Jerusalem. And he has come here
                with authority from the chief priests to arrest
                all who call on your name.

NARR: (*Sternly*) But the Lord said to Ananias, 'Go!
                This man is my chosen instrument to carry my
                name before the Gentiles and their kings and
                before the people of Israel. I will show him how
                much he must suffer for my name.'

(ANANIAS *succumbs and walks tentatively towards* SAUL.)

                Then Ananias went to the house and entered it.
                Placing his hands on Saul, he said,

ANANIAS: (*Nervously*) Brother Saul, the Lord – Jesus, who
                appeared to you on the road as you were
                coming here – has sent me so that you may see
                again and be filled with the Holy Spirit.

NARR: (*With urgency in voice*) Immediately, something like scales fell from Saul's eyes, and he could see again.

(SAUL *smiles as he realises his sight is back. He looks at* ANANIAS *and stands full height, much to* ANANIAS*'s concern.* SAUL *stretches out his arms to embrace a relieved* ANANIAS.)

He got up and was baptised, and after taking some food, he regained his strength.

(SAUL *exits with arm around* ANANIAS.)

44. Paul and Silas in Prison

IN A NUTSHELL

Earlier I mentioned that I collated many of the passages in this book through a voting system of esteemed friends and colleagues. This short section was one that came very high on that final list.

While on his second missionary journey accompanied by Silas, Paul is thrown into prison, a peaceful man treated like the worst of criminals. It serves as an example to us to praise God in all circumstances, as he will help us overcome. That can sound rather trite when we are faced with life's difficulties, but the impact of this passage is totally inspiring. Even after he is given the means to escape from prison, Paul elects to stay, ministering to the jailer and ultimately proving a point to the authorities.

I have scripted this for a narrator and three actors. Using minimal effort with sound, light and props, try to conjure up the dank cell for the audience.

Cast: NARRATOR, PAUL, SILAS, JAILER.

Props: Sound FX: sad music; earthquake and falling buildings. Lights. Chains/rope. Chair. Apple. Sword.

THE READING

(*Darkness. Sad music is heard and lights go up on* JAILER, *with* PAUL *and* SILAS *either side of him, severely beaten. He pushes them to the floor, securing their feet, and takes his place on a*

201

chair to the side, relaxing and eating an apple. Music fades, quietly playing underneath narration.)

NARR: The crowd joined in the attack against Paul and Silas, and the magistrates ordered them to be stripped and beaten. After they had been severely flogged, they were thrown into prison, and the jailer was commanded to guard them carefully. Upon receiving such orders, he put them in the inner cell and fastened their feet in the stocks.

(*As music fades to silence,* PAUL *and* SILAS *quietly sing a hymn or song.*)

               About midnight Paul and Silas were praying and singing hymns to God, and the other prisoners were listening to them.

                    (*Quickening tempo*) Suddenly there was such a violent earthquake that the foundations of the prison were shaken. (*Sound FX: earthquake, destruction*) At once all the prison doors flew open, and everybody's chains came loose. The jailer woke up, and when he saw the prison doors open, he drew his sword and was about to kill himself because he thought the prisoners had escaped. But Paul shouted,

PAUL: (*Shouts*) Don't harm yourself! We are all here!

(JAILER *stops, sword raised.*)

NARR: The jailer called for lights, rushed in and fell trembling before Paul and Silas. He then brought them out and asked,

JAILER: (*Sitting with* PAUL *and* SILAS *on floor*) Sirs, what must I do to be saved?

PAUL: Believe in the Lord Jesus, and you will be saved
          – you and your household.

NARR: Then they spoke the word of the Lord to him
          and to all the others in his house.

45. Dead to Sin, Alive in Christ

IN A NUTSHELL

In his famous letter to the church in Rome, Paul gives a brilliant overview of what he will be preaching ahead of his arrival. Chapter 6 speaks of how Christ completely breaks the power sin has over us. Whatever we do, it is impossible for God to love us less – he will always forgive. At the same time, though, he rejects the notion that we can continue sinning, stating that we are now living a new life in Christ, dead to sin.

It is a wonderful passage, and in preparation I would suggest reading it through numerous times, catching the infectious verve Paul has for what he is saying. Once you have done this, I think you will agree it is not a piece to read in a staid or monotone fashion, but with passion and excitement. I have scripted it for a solo reader, giving a variety of directions for vocal tones to help you understand just how Paul himself might have delivered it.

Cast: PAUL.

Props: None required.

THE READING

PAUL: (*Questioning audience*) What shall we say, then? (*Pause for response*) Shall we go on sinning, so that grace may increase? (*Pause again, then dismissive, mocking*) By no means!

(*With unbelief*) We died to sin; how can we live in it any longer?

(*As if suddenly realising the listener may not understand*) Or don't you know that all of us who were baptised into Christ Jesus were baptised into his death?

We were therefore buried with him through baptism into death in order that, just as Christ was raised from the dead through the glory of the Father, we too may live a new life. (*Ends on a note of amazement*)

(*Explains further for those still not with him*) If we have been united with him like this in his death, we will certainly also be united with him in his resurrection. For we know that our old self was crucified with him so that the body of sin might be done away with, that we should no longer be slaves to sin – because anyone who has died has been freed from sin.

(*And once more explains the scenario*) Now if we died with Christ, we believe that we will also live with him. (*Uses arms to demonstrate resurrection*) For we know that since Christ was raised from the dead, he cannot die again; death no longer has mastery over him. The death he died, he died to sin once for all; but the life he lives, (*Pause*) he lives to God.

(*Pauses to smile and look around congregation, joyfully including everyone in his revelation*) In the same way, count yourselves dead to sin but alive to God in Christ Jesus. (*Rejecting tones*) Therefore do not let sin reign in your mortal body so that you obey its evil desires. Do not offer the parts of your body to sin, as instruments of wickedness, (*With lighter, joyful tones*) but rather offer yourselves to God, as those who have been brought from death to life; and offer the parts of your body to him as instruments of righteousness.

(*Final words of encouragement*) For sin shall not be your master, because you are not under law, (*Pause*) but under grace.

NOTES

When we speak of dramatising Scripture, it does not always mean we use a number of readers or set up a mini play. One of my favourite forms of drama is the monologue, which has an unparalleled ability to peel back the surface of a character and get right under their skin. It is also probably the most difficult style of drama to perform – by its very definition, you are on your own! Similarly, with a dramatised reading for a solo reader, don't automatically assume it's easy. You have the job of communicating a truth, an opinion and a character's feeling. Take time to understand the text and where the writer was coming from. The emotion will often be unwritten but clear in the subtext, and you must read between the lines in order to communicate this too.

46. Life Through the Spirit

IN A NUTSHELL

This passage, also written for a single reader, is very much a companion to the selection from Romans 6. There Paul speaks of how Christ broke the power of sin; here we see how a Christian can live that life of victory over sin through the Spirit. We have a choice to make: to be controlled by our sinful nature, doing what we want to do, or to be controlled by the Holy Spirit, doing what Christ would have us do. Once we decide to follow Christ and discover the peace it brings, we should make a conscious choice daily to follow him, so that selfish desires will not survive. Obviously, it is often easier said than done, yet if we believe that the power that caused Christ to rise from the dead is available to us, the problems will not seem so insurmountable.

As with the previous passage, it will help you to picture how Paul would have verbalised this part of the letter if you read it through several times. We know he was a powerful communicator, so it would certainly have been infectious and challenging.

Cast: PAUL.

Props: Desk and chair. Paper and pen.

THE READING

(PAUL *is writing at his desk, adding final touches to his letter. He stands in excitement to speak. The first part of the reading*

207

*is spoken with an agitated excitement; his thoughts are flood-
ing out wildly in his verve to tell the good news.*)

PAUL: (*Reading*) Therefore, there is now no condem-
                nation for those who are in Christ Jesus,
                because through Christ Jesus the law of the
                Spirit of life set me free from the law of sin and
                death. For what the law was powerless to do
                (*Voice drops as an aside*) in that it was weakened
                by the sinful nature, (*Back to declaring voice*)
                God did by sending his own Son in the likeness
                of sinful man to be a sin offering. (*Adding
                quickly, as if he nearly forgot to say*) And so he
                condemned sin in sinful man, (*Again quickly
                adds the explanation*) in order that the right-
                eous requirements of the law might be fully met
                in us, who do not live according to the sinful
                nature but according to the Spirit.

(*After his opening flurry,* PAUL *pauses to concentrate, checking
his letter. He then focuses on communicating clearly and
simply what he wants to say.* PAUL *compares people living by
the sinful nature to those living by the Spirit. To define the two
clearly, he physically turns one way for sinful, the other way for
spiritual. He also changes vocal tones, using negative tones for
sinful, positive tones for spiritual.*)

                (*Turns, negative*) Those who live according to
                the sinful nature have their minds set on what
                that nature desires; (*Turns, positive*) but those
                who live in accordance with the Spirit have
                their minds set on what the Spirit desires.
                    (*Turns, negative*) The mind of sinful man is
                death, (*Turns, positive*) but the mind controlled
                by the Spirit is life and peace; (*Turns, negative*)

the sinful mind is hostile to God. It does not submit to God's law, nor can it do so. Those controlled by the sinful nature cannot please God. (*Turns, positive*) You, however, are controlled not by the sinful nature but by the Spirit, if the Spirit of God lives in you.

(*Declares to wider audience*) And if anyone does not have the Spirit of Christ, he does not belong to Christ.

(*With increasing excitement*) But if Christ is in you, your body is dead because of sin, yet your spirit is alive because of righteousness. And if the Spirit of him who raised Jesus from the dead is living in you, he who raised Christ from the dead will also give life to your mortal bodies through his Spirit, who lives in you. (*Visibly puffs, amazed by the truth spoken. He sits down, seriously worn out*)

(*Pause, then calmly*) Therefore, brothers, we have an obligation — but it is not to the sinful nature, to live according to it. For if you live according to the sinful nature, (*Pause*) you will die; but if by the Spirit you put to death the misdeeds of the body, you will live, because those who are led by the Spirit of God arc sons of God.

For you did not receive a spirit that makes you a slave again to fear, but you received the Spirit of sonship. And by him we cry, '*Abba*, Father.' The Spirit himself testifies with our spirit that we are God's children. Now if we are children, then we are heirs – heirs of God and co-heirs with Christ, if indeed we share in his sufferings in order that we may also share in his glory.

47. Love

IN A NUTSHELL

This passage must be one of the most famous in the pages of the Bible, and anyone, regardless of his or her personal belief, can marvel at its beauty. The meaning of true love is a conundrum with which mere mortal man struggles to come to terms; here we have a wonderful definition of what love really is.

The passage is often chosen at weddings, and I have had the privilege of reading it at quite a few. Particularly in a wedding situation, imagine that you are speaking it personally to the happy couple. Okay, we know it's actually a critical letter from Paul to the church at Corinth, but it is no less a message for us today, and what more important message could there be for newlyweds? Spoken from the heart, it touches on the divine.

Cast: READER.

Props: None required.

THE READING

(*Spoken as yourself, directed at gathered congregation or, in the case of a wedding, directly to the couple.*)

READER: (*Conspiratorially, as if letting congregation in on a great secret*) And now I will show you the most excellent way.

(*Pause*) If I speak in the tongues of men and of angels, but have not love, (*Downbeat*) I am only a resounding gong or a clanging cymbal.

(*Bewildered*) If I have the gift of prophecy and can fathom all mysteries and all knowledge, and I have a faith that can move mountains, but have not love, (*Deflated*) I am nothing.

(*Earnestly*) If I give all I possess to the poor and surrender my body to the flames, but have not love, (*Once more deflated*) I gain nothing.

(*Pause, thoughtfully describing*) Love is (*Pause*) patient, love is kind. It does not envy, it does not boast, it is not proud. It is not rude, it is not self-seeking, it is not easily angered, it keeps no record of wrongs. Love does not delight in evil but rejoices with the truth. It always protects, always trusts, always hopes, always perseveres. Love never fails.

(*Pause for change of thought. With upward intonation*) But where there are prophecies, (*Downward intonation*) they will cease; (*Upward intonation*) where there are tongues, (*Downward intonation*) they will be stilled; (*Upward intonation*) where there is knowledge, (*Downward intonation*) it will pass away.

(*Explaining mode*) For we know in part and we prophesy in part, but when perfection comes, the imperfect disappears.

(*As if explaining more clearly the previous conundrum*) When I was a child, I talked like a child, I thought like a child, I reasoned like a child. (*With masculine deep voice*) When I became a man, I put childish ways behind me.

(*Smiling and spoken quietly*) Now we see but a poor reflection as in a mirror; then we shall see face to face. Now I know in part; then I shall know fully, even as I am fully known.

(*Pause, summing up*) And now these three remain: faith, hope and love. But the greatest of these (*Pause*) is love.

48. The Armour of God

IN A NUTSHELL

This passage describing the armour of God is one where I feel pulled in two directions as to its best mode of communication. It so obviously lends itself to a visual presentation, with a clear indication of what each item of armour represents. On the other hand, does dressing someone up in a mock suit of armour actually invite unwanted laughter, serving only to detract from the powerful message?

I think the answer lies in the audience to whom you will be reading. Clearly at a fun family service the visual images will help, especially if they are used in the teaching that follows. However, at a predominantly adult gathering, it may come over as rather basic to use a costume instead of the powerful images of the words alone.

For this script, I have assumed a family service scenario, using a basic version to illustrate the point. An essential point to communicate is the necessity for the *whole* armour: if any part is lacking, we are a sitting duck for the enemy's blazing arrows.

Cast: NARRATOR, SOLDIER, DRESSER.

Props: Sound FX: trumpet fanfare. Lights. Armour: belt, breastplate, boots, shield, helmet, sword.

THE READING

(Music: trumpet sound or some form of call to battle. Lights up on SOLDIER *and* DRESSER *in frozen position.* SOLDIER *seated regally;* DRESSER *kneeling at his side.)*

NARR: Finally, be strong in the Lord and in his mighty power. Put on the full armour of God so that you can take your stand against the devil's schemes. For our struggle is not against flesh and blood, but against the rulers, against the authorities, against the powers of this dark world and against the spiritual forces of evil in the heavenly realms.

Therefore put on the full armour of God, so that when the day of evil comes, you may be able to stand your ground, and after you have done everything, to stand.

(As if speaking to SOLDIER*, who at the word 'stand' gets up)* Stand firm then, with the belt of truth buckled round your waist,

*(*DRESSER *puts belt round* SOLDIER*'s waist. He fastens it too tight and loosens it at the* SOLDIER*'s pained beckoning.)*

with the breastplate of righteousness in place,

*(*DRESSER *places breastplate over* SOLDIER*'s head.)*

and with your feet fitted with the readiness that comes from the gospel of peace.

*(*SOLDIER *slips his feet into pre-positioned boots.)*

In addition to all this, take up the shield of faith, with which you can extinguish all the flaming arrows of the evil one.

(DRESSER *hands* SOLDIER *a shield.*)

> Take the helmet of salvation and the sword of
> the Spirit, which is the word of God.

(DRESSER *positions helmet on* SOLDIER*'s head and hands him
the sword.*)

> And pray in the Spirit on all occasions with all
> kinds of prayers and requests.

(*By this point* DRESSER *and* SOLDIER *should be back in frozen
positions.*)

> With this in mind, be alert and always keep on
> praying for all the saints.

NOTES

This is a very basic, and arguably childish, way to illustrate
the armour of God, but it will serve to make the point effectively. To best perform this, the dresser and soldier need to
rehearse slick movements for putting on the armour. If they
are clumsy about it, the whole thing will be spun out and
messy and will spoil the flow of the reading. So although the
roles are unspoken, they will need to be run through. Take
some time to create effective props – in this particular
reading the props are the focal point.

To best use the images shown in the reading, the teacher
could go on to use the props as visual aids to make the point
of their varying uses. It might seem a very obvious point, but
it will really help the teaching to sink in. As mentioned in the
introduction, this style of reading and teaching is best suited
to a family service.

49. Imitating Christ's Humility

IN A NUTSHELL

This passage is taken from Paul's letter to the church at Philippi, and is one of my favourite biblical letters. I find it very thought-provoking and personally challenging, not least because Paul penned it from inside a prison cell. The underlying message of joy shines through Paul's words.

In this section of the letter, Paul implores us to love and serve other believers (even the ones we don't especially like!), challenging us with the aim of imitating the humility of Christ. Because of what Christ has done for us – 'therefore' (v. 12) – we should adopt a lifestyle of humble service, not selfish ambition. Not only do we need to serve, we need to do it with the right motives, not 'complaining and arguing' or seeking only to give a good outward impression.

When vocalising Paul's letter, it is easy to slip into reading it rather morosely and with furrowed brow because of its serious nature and his imprisonment. Of course we need to give the words their due weight, but it is also essential to communicate Paul's incredible joy.

Cast: READER, JESUS (non-speaking part).

Props: Sound FX: prison doors slamming, chains rattling; opening music; bass drumbeat; soft music. Desk and two chairs. Pen and paper. Handful of sand or soil. Stepladder (optional).

THE READING

(Opening music, with sound FX of prison doors slamming, chains rattling, if possible. PAUL *is sitting at a desk writing. A man sits silently next to him, later revealed to be* JESUS, *signifying his constant presence with* PAUL. *The reading is essentially in the style of* PAUL *checking over the content of his letter.)*

PAUL: *(Short silent pause after music. He reads each phrase as if to the recipient, pausing between each for thought)* If you have any encouragement from being united with Christ, *(Pause)* if any comfort from his love, *(Pause)* if any fellowship with the Spirit, *(Pause)* if any tenderness and compassion, *(Pause)* then make my joy complete by being like-minded, having the same love, being one in spirit and purpose.

(Stands and continues to read) Do nothing out of selfish ambition or vain conceit, but in humility consider others better than yourselves. Each of you should look not only to your own interests, but also to the interests of others.

Your attitude should be the same as that of Christ Jesus:

(As soon as his name is mentioned, JESUS *stands and slowly moves to centre stage.)*

Who, being in very nature God, did not consider equality with God something to be grasped,

(By this point JESUS *should have reached centre stage and be standing still, eyes focused heavenwards.)*

but made himself nothing,

(JESUS *lets sand or soil slip slowly from his clenched fists to the floor.*)

taking the very nature of a servant, being made in human likeness. And being found in appearance as a man, he humbled himself and became obedient to death –

(*Sound FX: loud bass drumbeat.* JESUS *throws his arms into cross position.*)

even death on a cross!

(*Pause. Soft music plays and* JESUS *slowly drops head, signifying death.*)

(*With increasing joy and excitement*) Therefore God exalted him to the highest place

(JESUS *moves to a high position – this is purely symbolic and can be anywhere, depending on your situation, perhaps an area of stage, a pulpit, a chair or stepladder.* PAUL *continues speaking during this movement. Once in position,* JESUS *focuses on* PAUL.)

and gave him the name that is above every name, that at the name of Jesus every knee should bow, (PAUL *falls to his knees holding on to his desk*) in heaven and on earth and under the earth, and every tongue confess that Jesus Christ is Lord, to the glory of God the Father.

(*Music fades out and* PAUL *pauses in deep wonder. He suddenly regains his train of thought and continues his speech and letter checking. Give weight to the 'therefore' which opens verse 12.*

It indicates PAUL*'s desire that the church should act in response to what Christ has done.*)

> Therefore, my dear friends, as you have always obeyed – not only in my presence, but now much more in my absence – continue to work out your salvation with fear and trembling, for it is God who works in you to will and to act according to his good purpose.
>
> (*Spoken with apparent disdain for the complainers and arguers*) Do everything without complaining or arguing, so that you may become blameless and pure, children of God without fault in a crooked and depraved generation, in which you shine like stars in the universe as you hold out the word of life – in order that I may boast on the day of Christ that I did not run or labour for nothing.
>
> But even if I am being poured out like a drink offering on the sacrifice and service coming from your faith, I am glad and rejoice with all of you. So you too should be glad and rejoice with me.

(PAUL, *apparently pleased, looks at his work smiling and laughing with contentment.* JESUS *is also smiling, looking at* PAUL. *Reprise of music to end.*)

50. Taming the Tongue

IN A NUTSHELL

People often desire the lofty position of teacher or preacher, but a quick glance at verse 1 here should be enough to put anyone off. As teachers, we are judged more strictly, our behaviour is there for all to see and compare to what we preach. The fact is, however, regardless of our official position, we all have much power in our tongues. It may be a small part of the body, but, like a ship's rudder, it has steering qualities.

Jesus suggests that no human can control this potential instrument of the devil, yet with the Holy Spirit guiding us we can begin to limit damage and use it in positive ways. We need to get ourselves to the place where, as soon as we use our tongue in unhealthy ways, the Spirit pricks our conscience and we learn the lesson. Scripted with suggestions for a powerful solo reading, this passage will challenge all who listen with an open mind.

Cast: JAMES.

Props: None required.

THE READING

JAMES: (*Warning tones*) Not many of you should presume to be teachers, my brothers, because you know that we who teach will be judged more strictly. We all stumble in many ways.

(*Spoken with slight sarcasm, as if asking someone to volunteer themselves as a perfect man*) If anyone is never at fault in what he says, he is a perfect man, able to keep his whole body in check.

(*Pause for response. Then, as if explaining*) When we put bits into the mouths of horses to make them obey us, we can turn the whole animal. (*Spoken as if* JAMES *has just thought of another example*) Or take ships as an example. Although they are so large and are driven by strong winds, they are steered by a very small rudder wherever the pilot wants to go.

(*Comparing, using opening warning tones*) Likewise the tongue is a small part of the body, but it makes great boasts. Consider what a great forest is set on fire by a small spark. (*Pause*) The tongue also is a fire, a world of evil among the parts of the body. (*With obvious distaste*) It corrupts the whole person, sets the whole course of his life on fire, and is itself set on fire by hell.

(*Lighter tones*) All kinds of animals, birds, reptiles and creatures of the sea are being tamed and have been tamed by man, (*Slight pause*) but no man can tame the tongue. (*Disdain returns*) It is a restless evil, full of deadly poison.

(*Thoughtfully and with a lighter tone*) With the tongue we praise our Lord and Father, (*Pause, darker tones*) and with it we curse men, who have been made in God's likeness. Out of the same mouth come praise and cursing.

(*Plea to congregation*) My brothers, this should not be. (*Rhetorical questions*) Can both fresh water and salt water flow from the same spring? My brothers, can a fig-tree bear olives, or a grapevine bear figs? (*Pause*) Neither can a salt spring produce fresh water.

Other books by David Burt...

50 Sketches about Jesus

Picture the scene: Jesus preaching at Wembley
Stadium; a paparazzi photographer in Bethlehem;
Mary cooking spaghetti hoops on toast; the wise men
shopping in Harrods. Strange? Maybe. Funny?
Certainly. But every sketch here highlights a truth
about Jesus of Nazareth that is relevant to life today.

There's something here for all levels of expertise, and
all ages. Fully indexed by themes, occasions and Bible
references, this is an ideal resource for churches and
other groups who wish to communicate old truths in
fresh ways.

25 Sketches about Proverbs

The book of Proverbs in the Bible has long been a
source of wit and wisdom for people of various ages,
races and cultures. So what better resource could we
have for creating funny but poignant sketches about
everyday life? From subjects as diverse as betrayal,
bullying, laziness and loneliness, there is something
here for everyone! Ideal for seeker-friendly services
and all-age worship.